AF521747

GIRL IN A GIRL BAND /

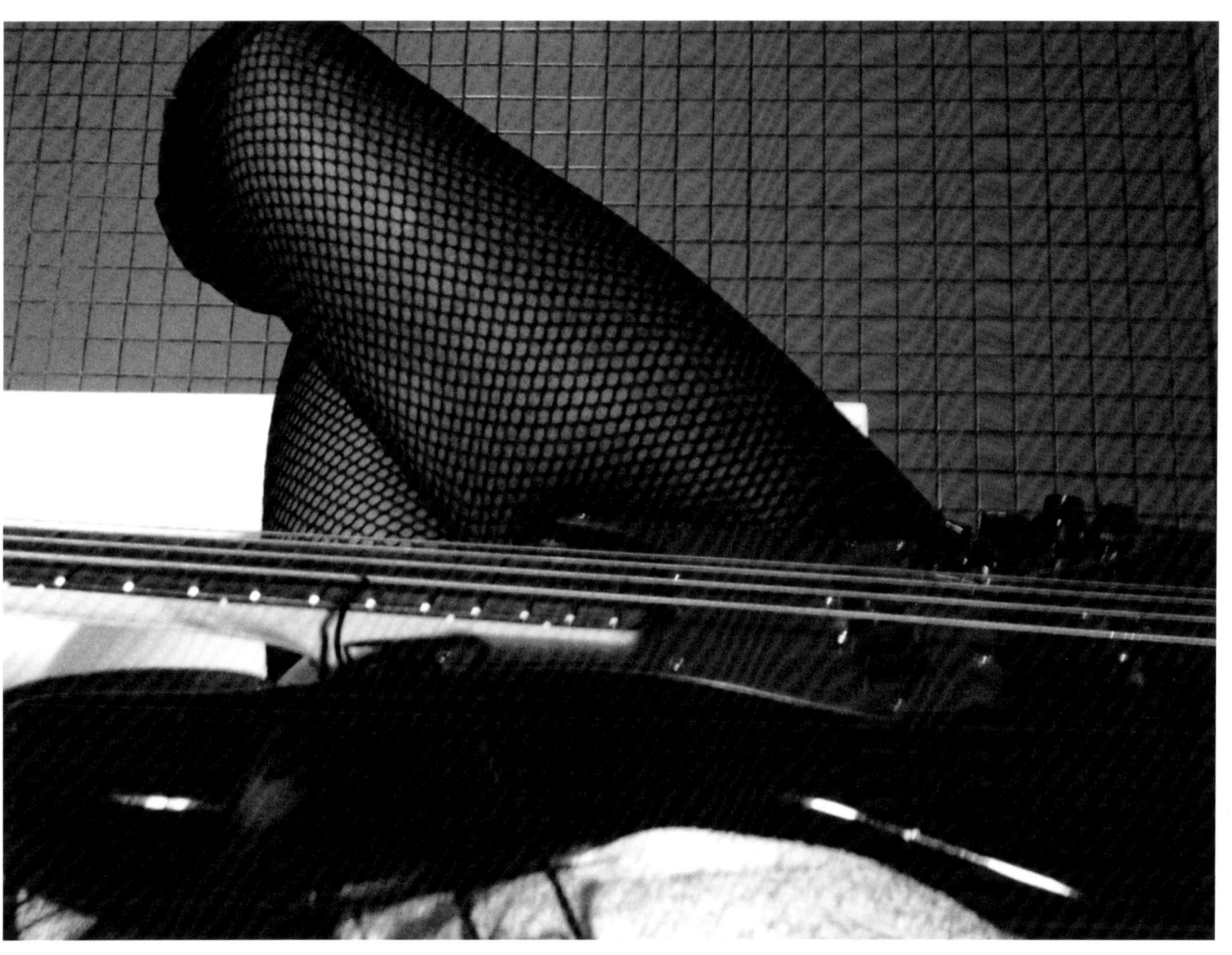

MALIA JAMES

GIRL IN A GIRL BAND /

MALIA JAMES

FOREWORD

I gave up on being a musician long before I started playing in bands. In fact, I tried and gave up many times. I resolved to being a kind of Annie Lewbotiz—someone who would commit my life to documenting music. And so, from a young age, I would jump into the van with anyone who would have me. At twenty-six, I moved to London on a whim. I didn't have a plan or much money, I just wanted to shake my life up a bit. Living there, I couldn't afford to do much, so I decided to finally commit to learning how to play an instrument. A friend I made there, KC Underwood, agreed to teach me. His bass player quit when they had shows booked, so I said, "teach me the bass and I'll be in your band." I started learning that day and played my first show to a packed house two weeks later. I toured for the next nine years of my life, playing music around the world.

There are a few images peppered in from my time on tour as a photographer, but the majority are from my time in Dum Dum Girls.

Being in a band is everything you dream it will be and nothing like you'd imagine. The highs are higher and the lows lower. When you're on the road, you're in a pack—in your own little bubble—and part of a tribe amongst other musicians. You're admitted purely by being in a one of them, but to be a girl in a girl band felt like having a special, unspeakable power.

Lust is easy to find and love is hard to maintain. On the last album cycle, we had our first Dum Dum Boy. And, for a time, we were a thing. I thought we'd be like Thurston and Kim, but the pressure cooker of being next to your person all day, every day, isn't something most relationships can withstand.

The world of life on the road looks different from the inside peering out. While you might expect a lot of sex, drugs, and rock n roll here, those are the moments you're too busy living to document when you're in it. Our time was a collection of early mornings, late nights, shared laughs, long drives, backstage dance parties, afternoon bike rides, hotel room drinks, and sleeping anywhere and any way we could in the van. Here you'll see my bandmates, our crew, tour mates, lovers that joined us on the road, and our lovers we found on the road. The rest are the textures of the ever-changing world around me.

Each picture was a way to remember every detail of a time I never want to forget and feel forever grateful to have lived.

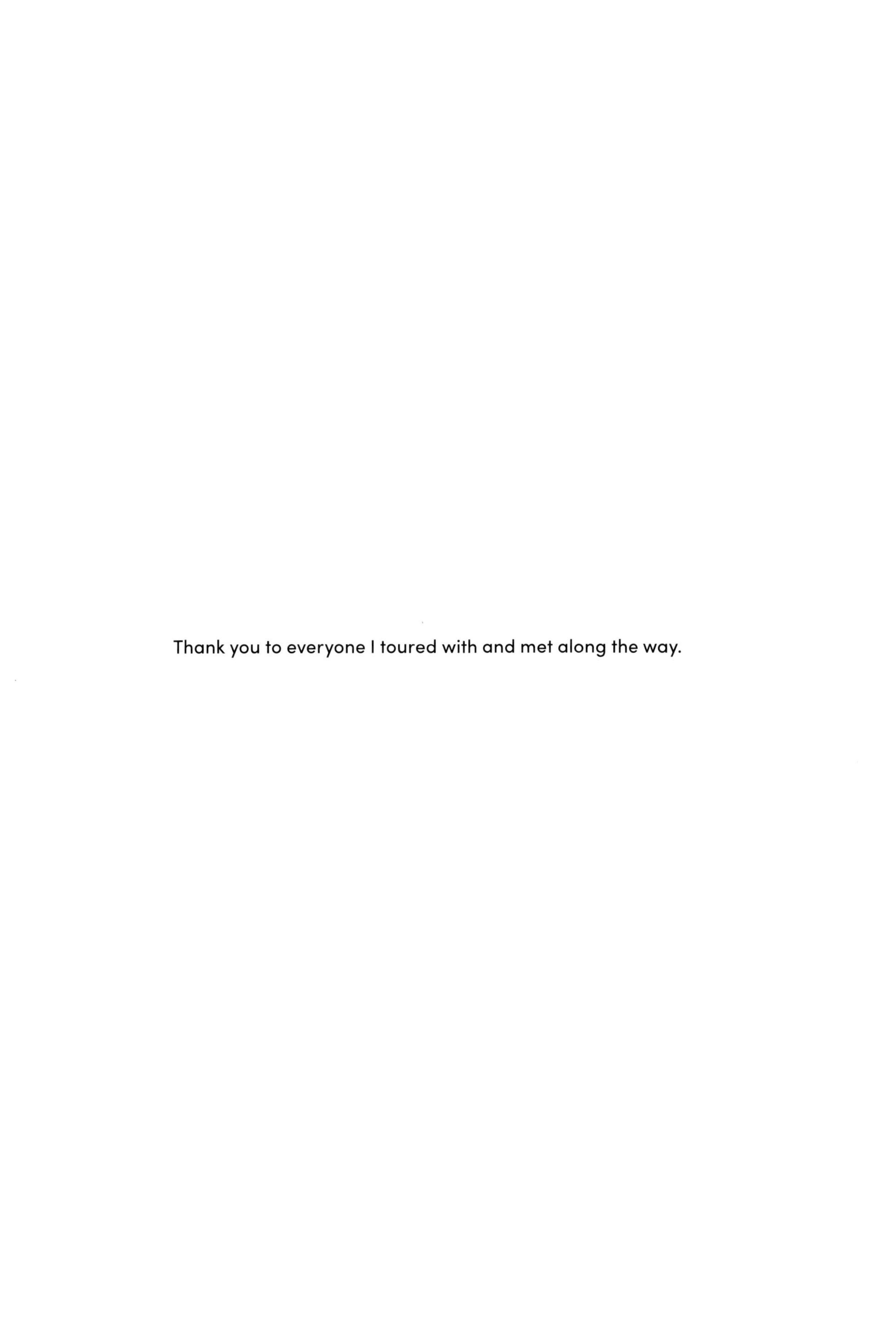

Thank you to everyone I toured with and met along the way.

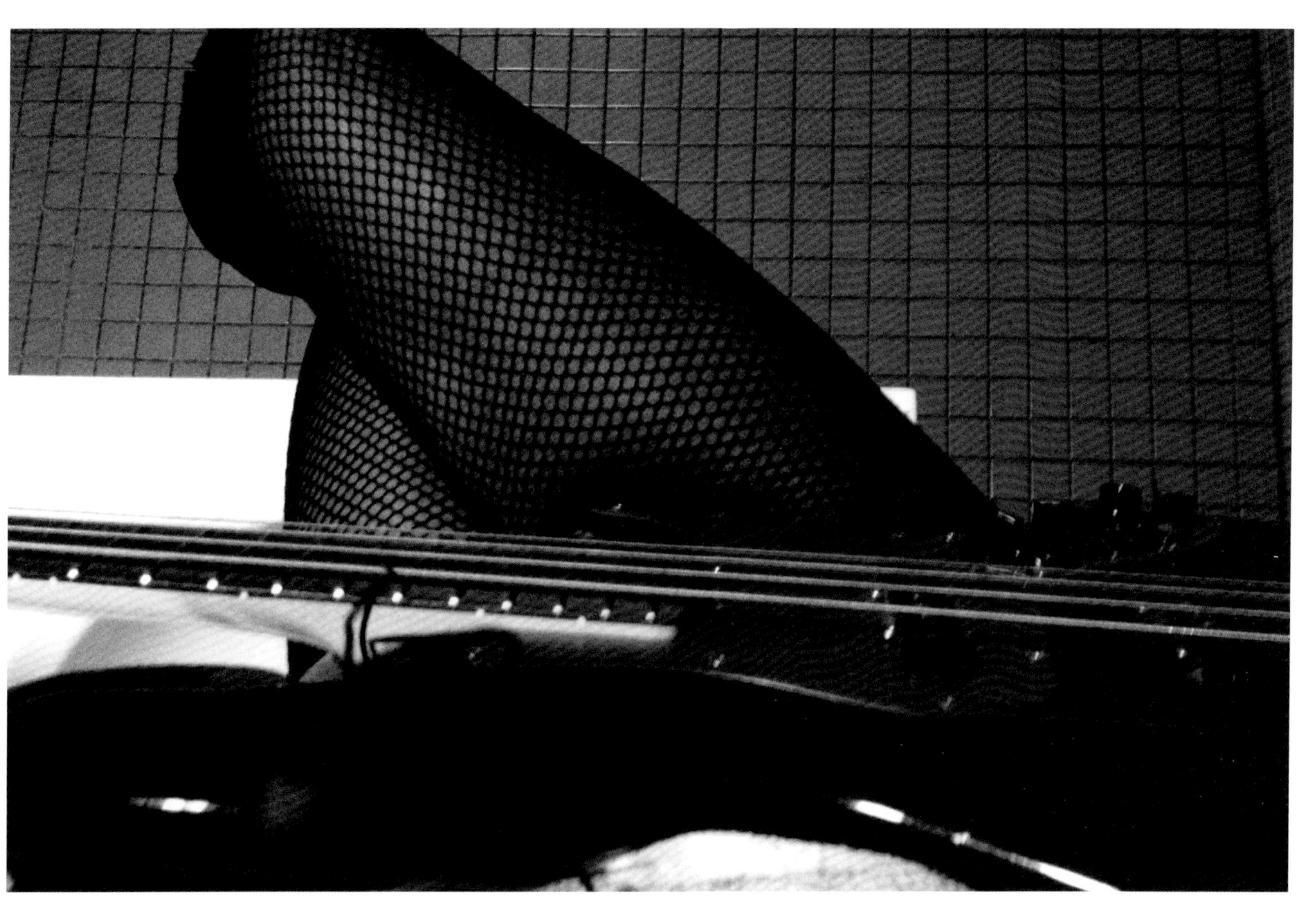

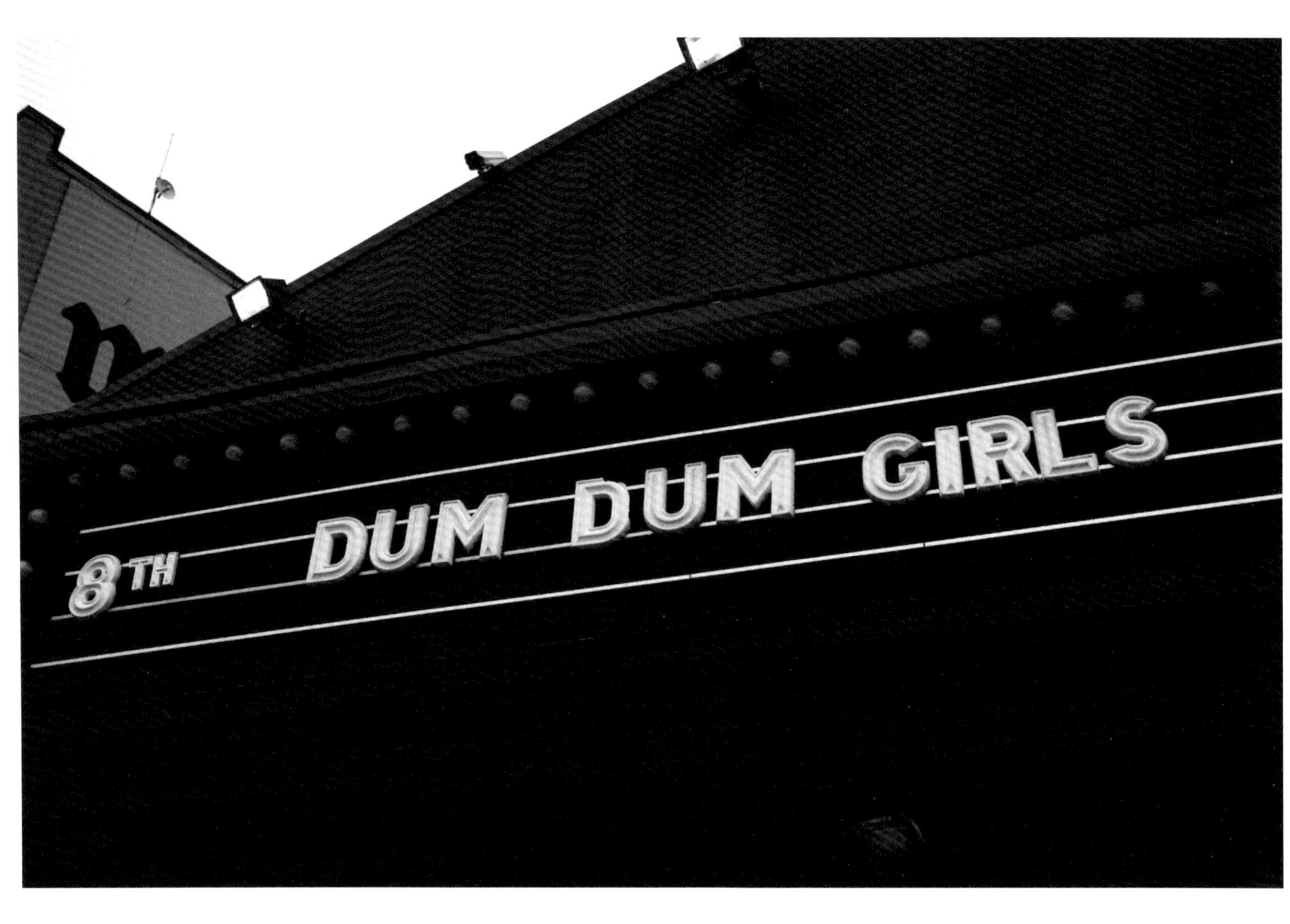
8TH
DUM DUM GIRLS

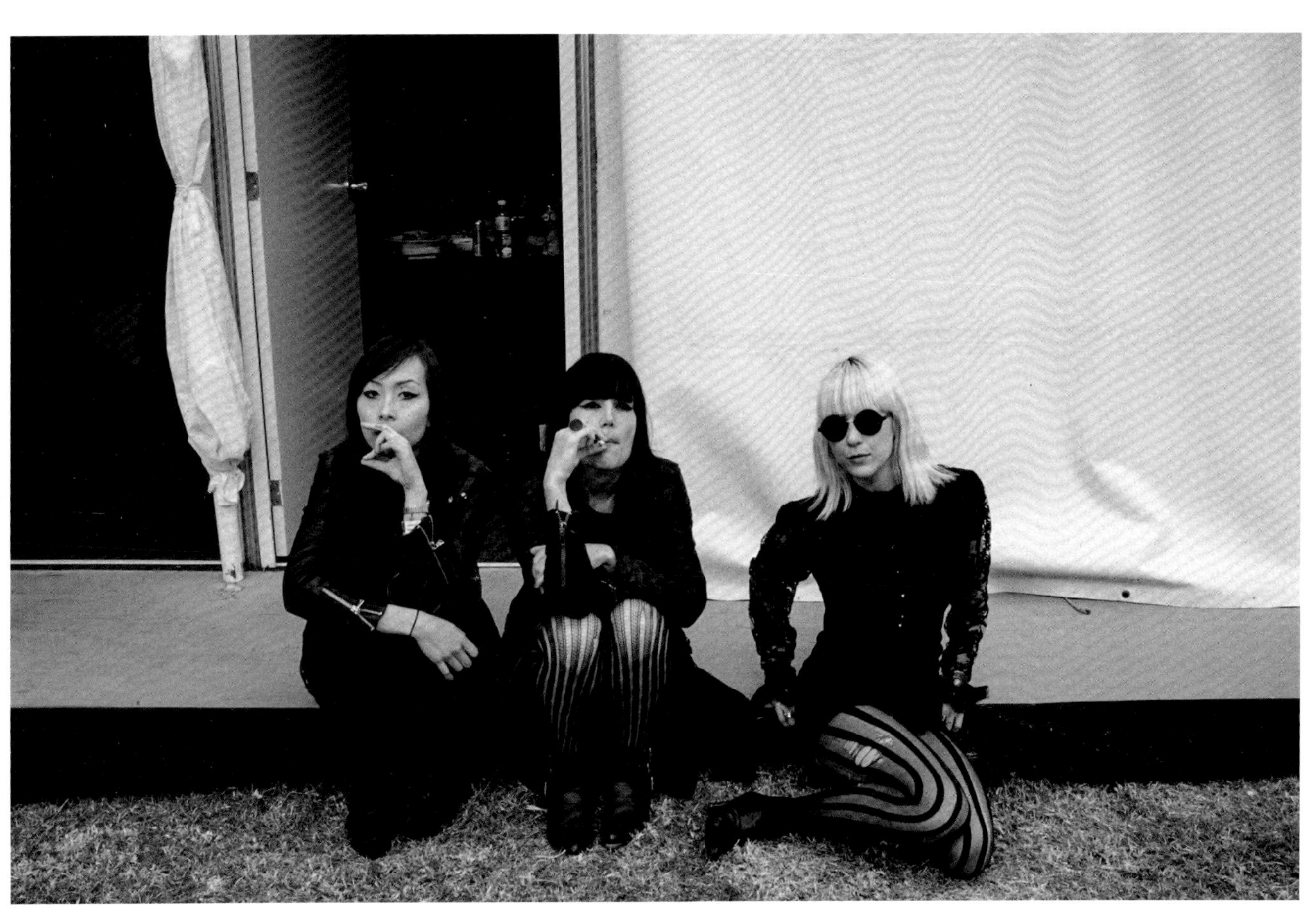

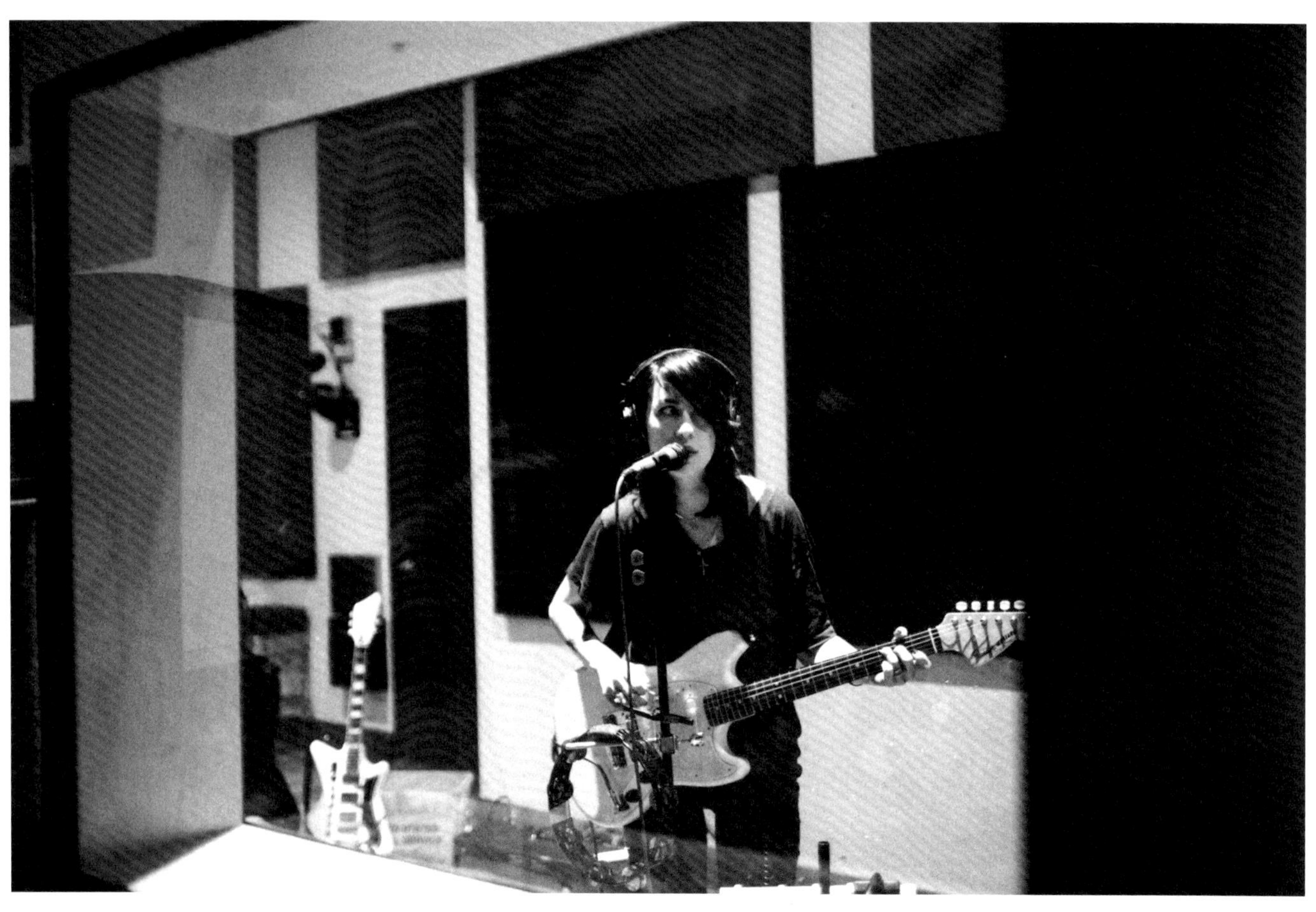

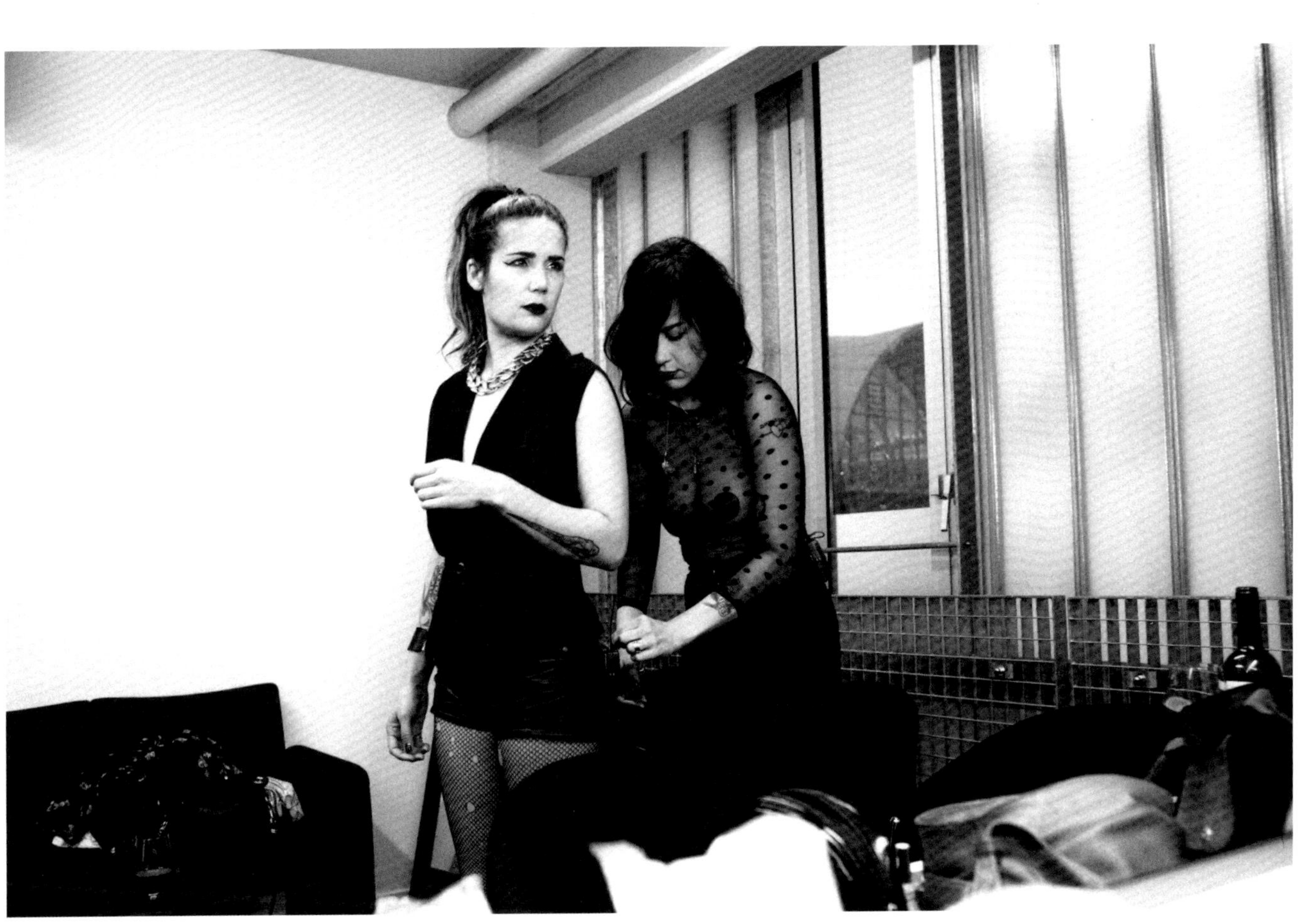

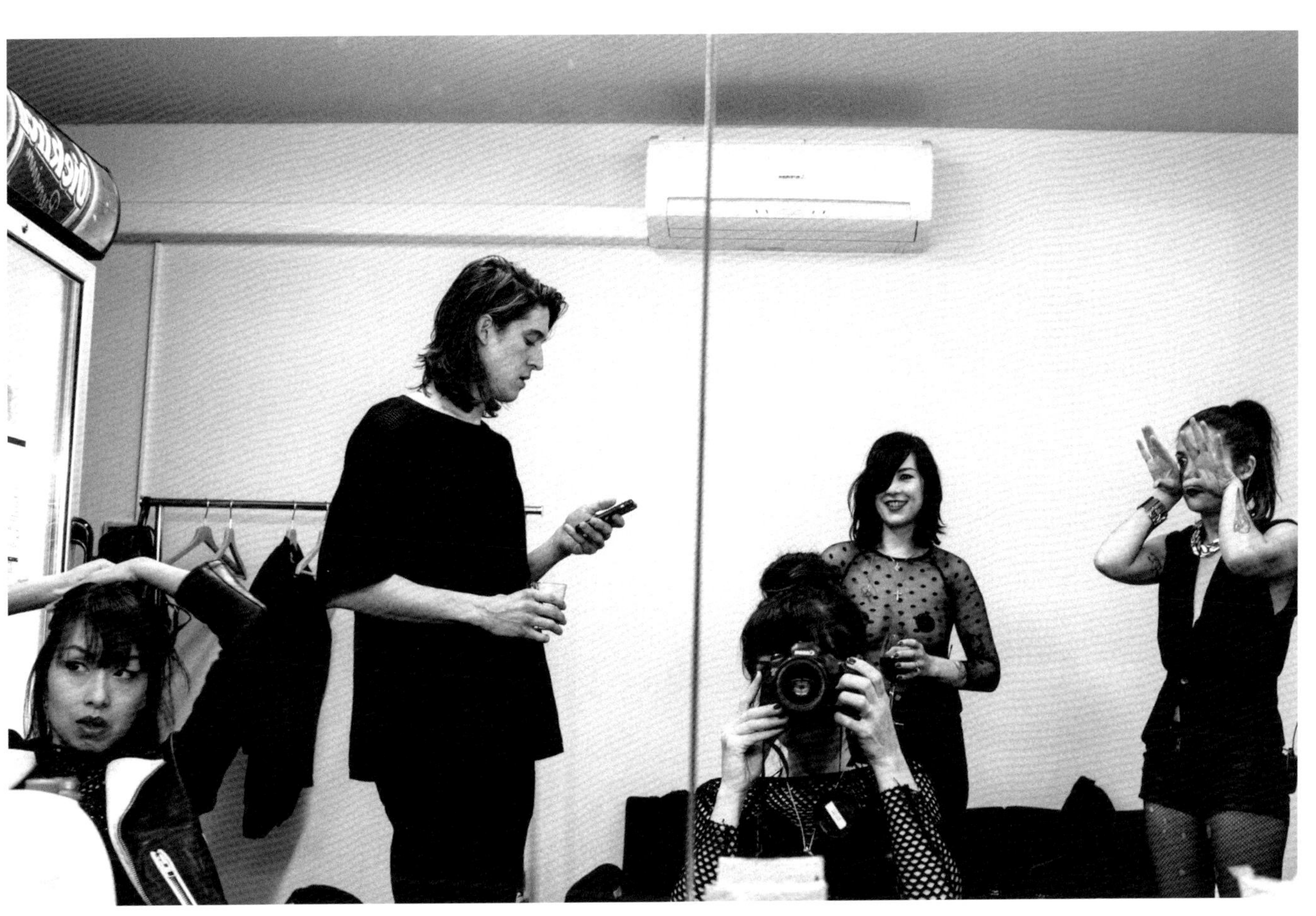

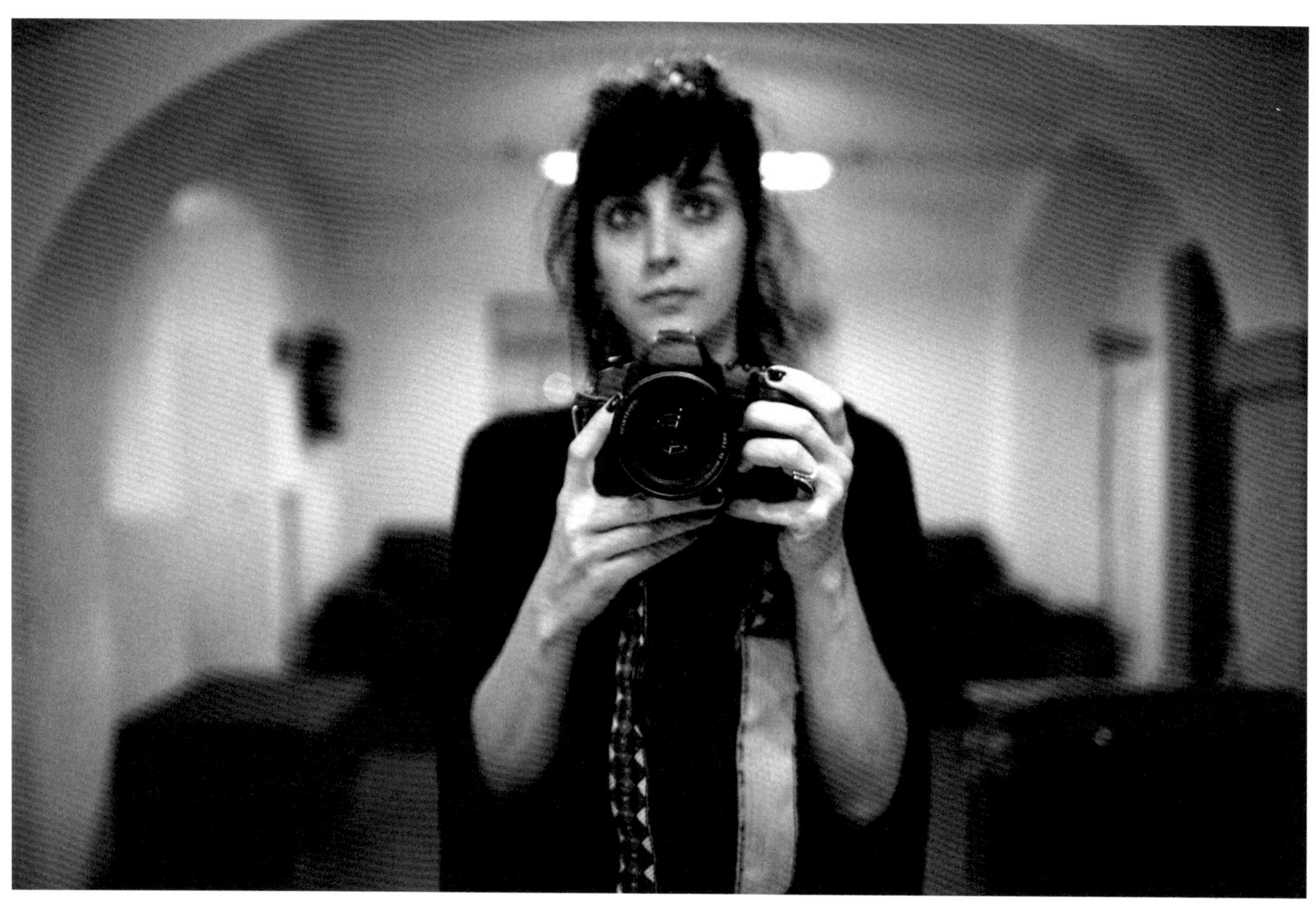

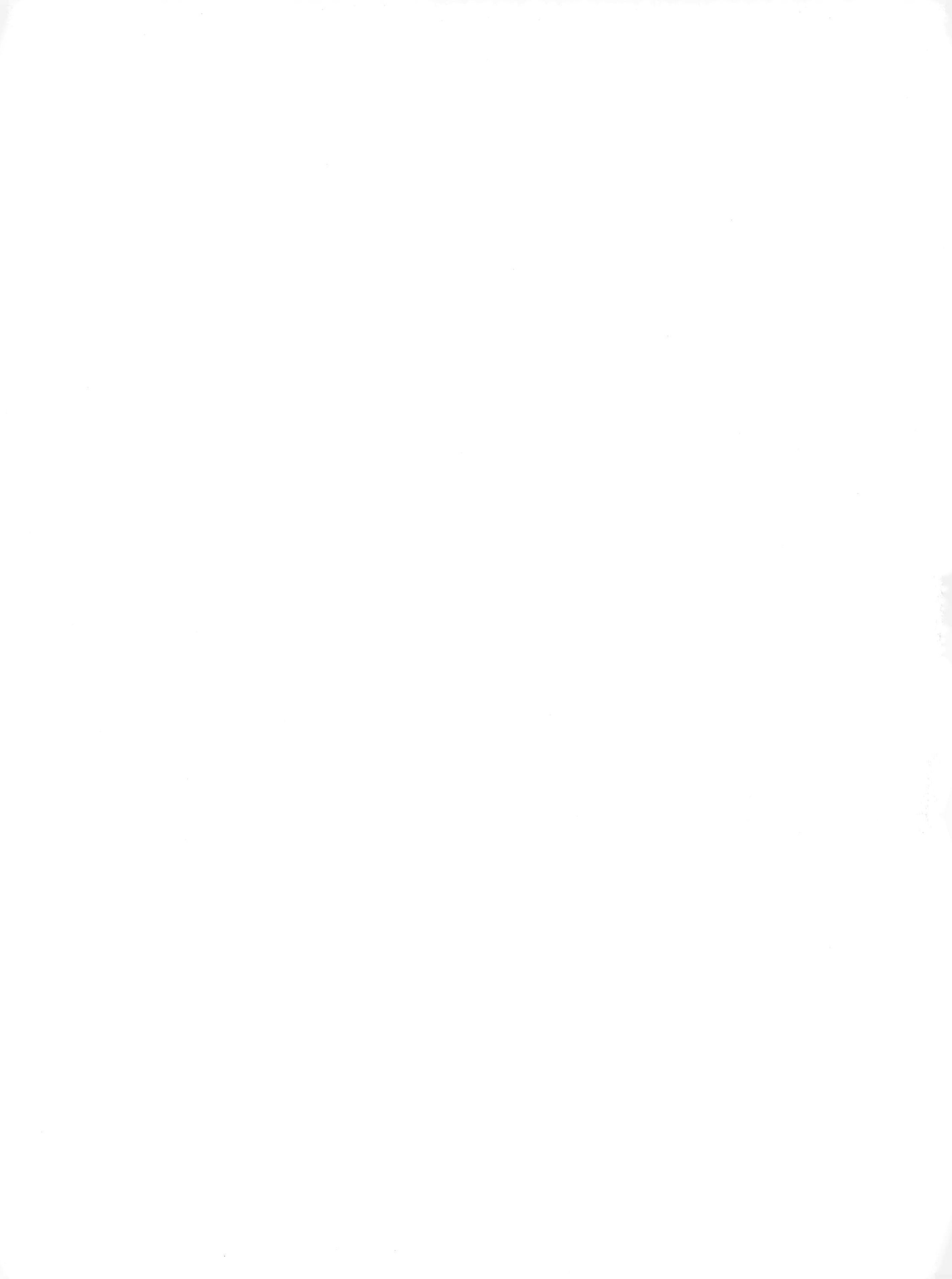

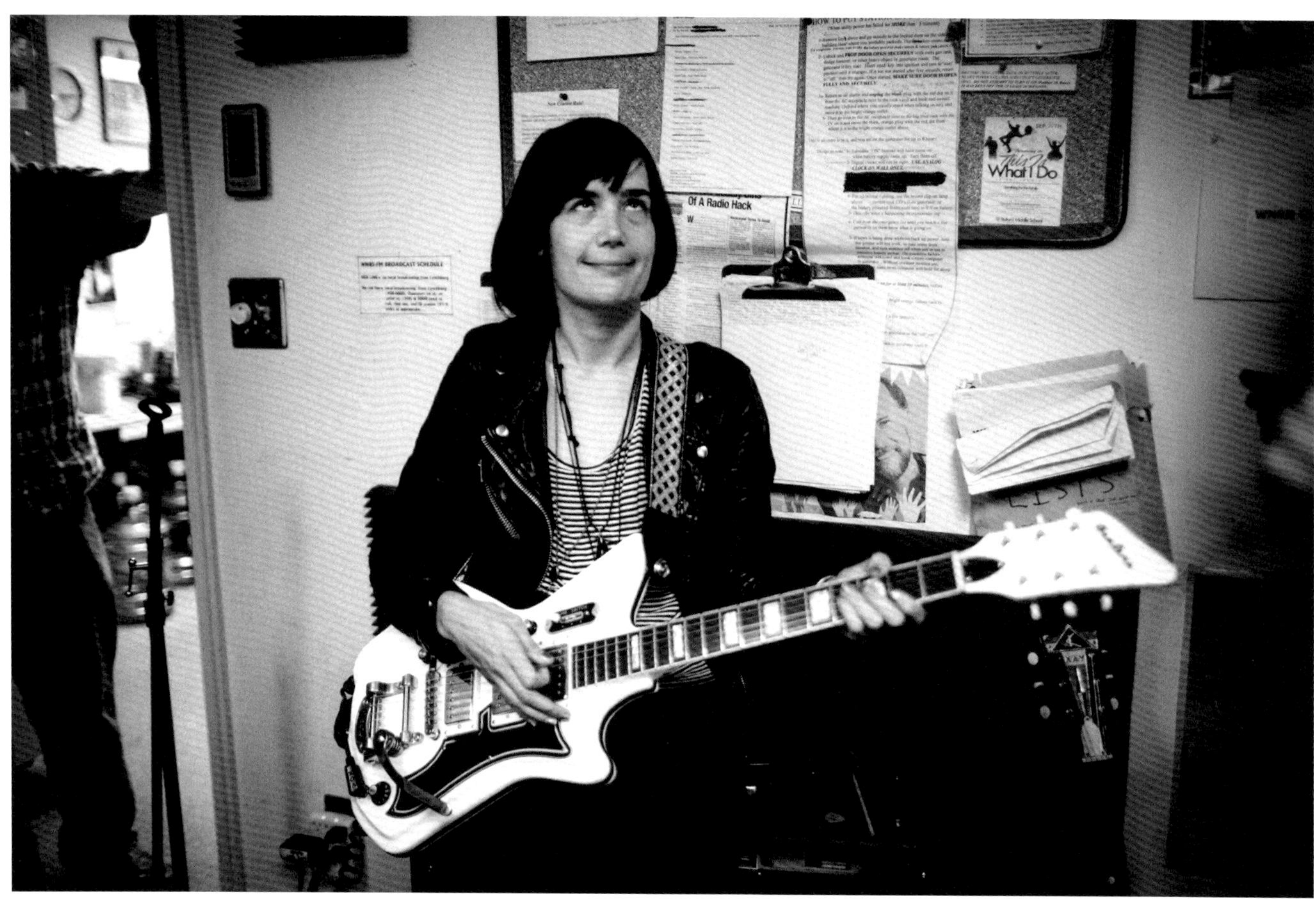
Of A Radio Hack
What I Do

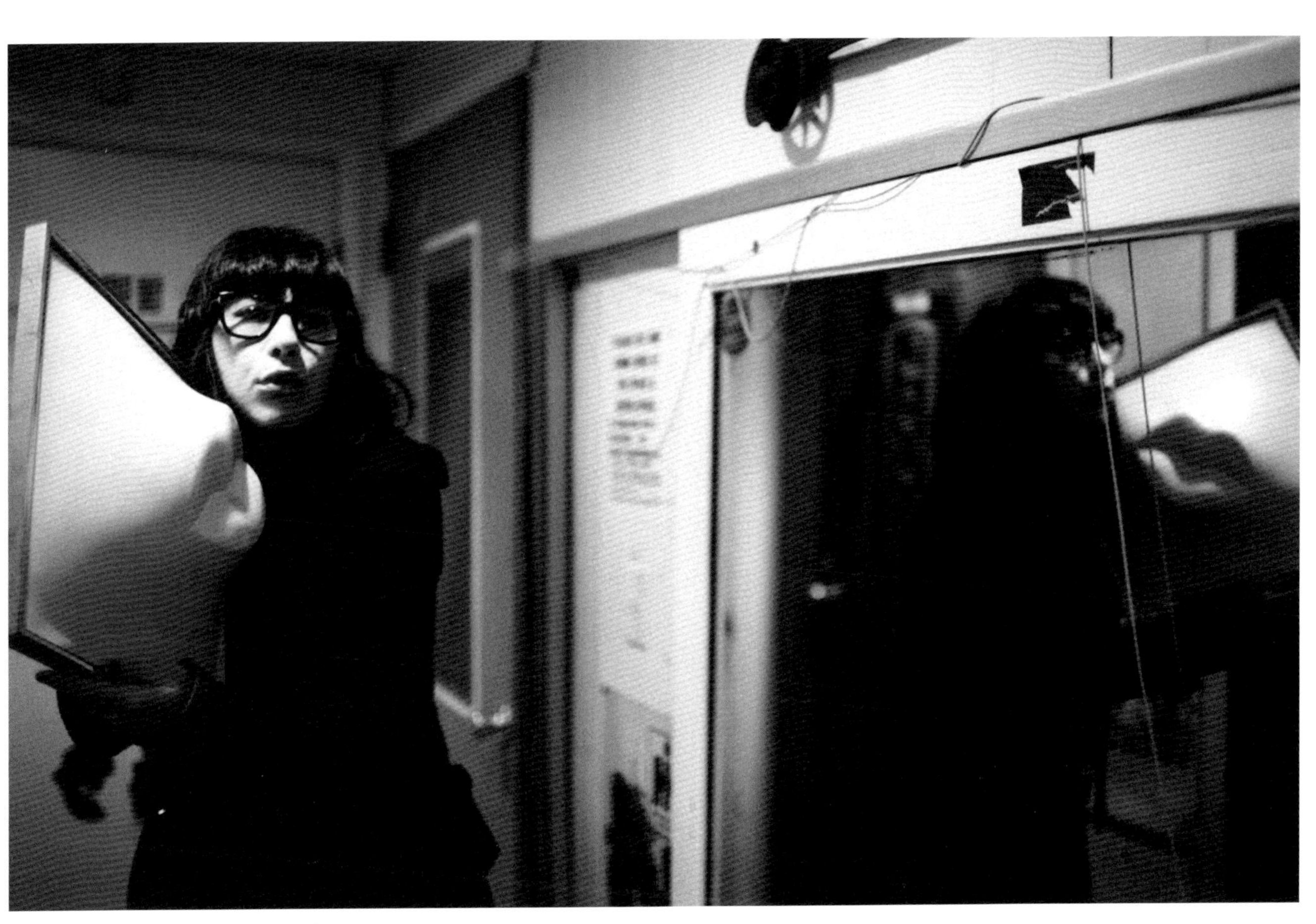

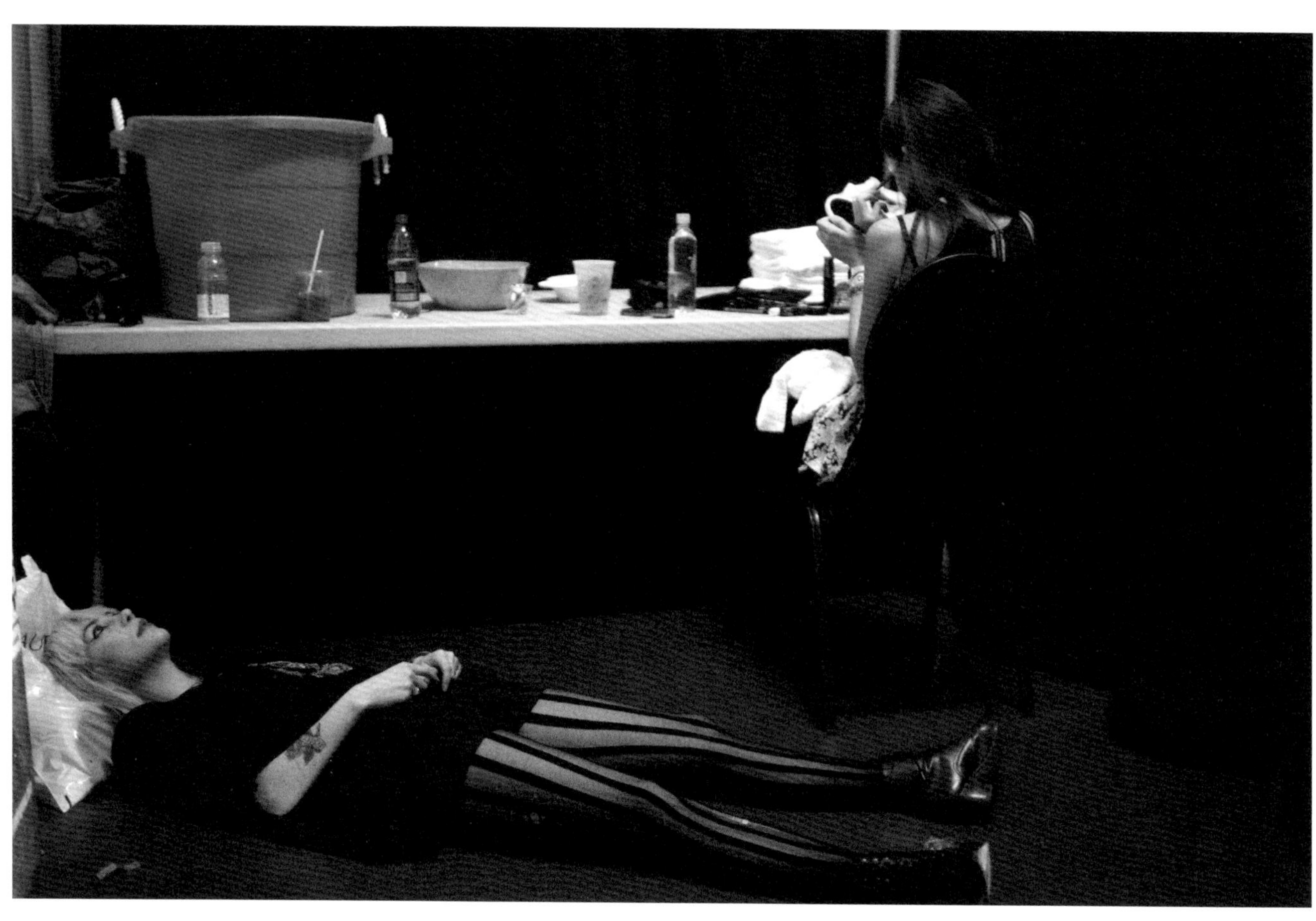

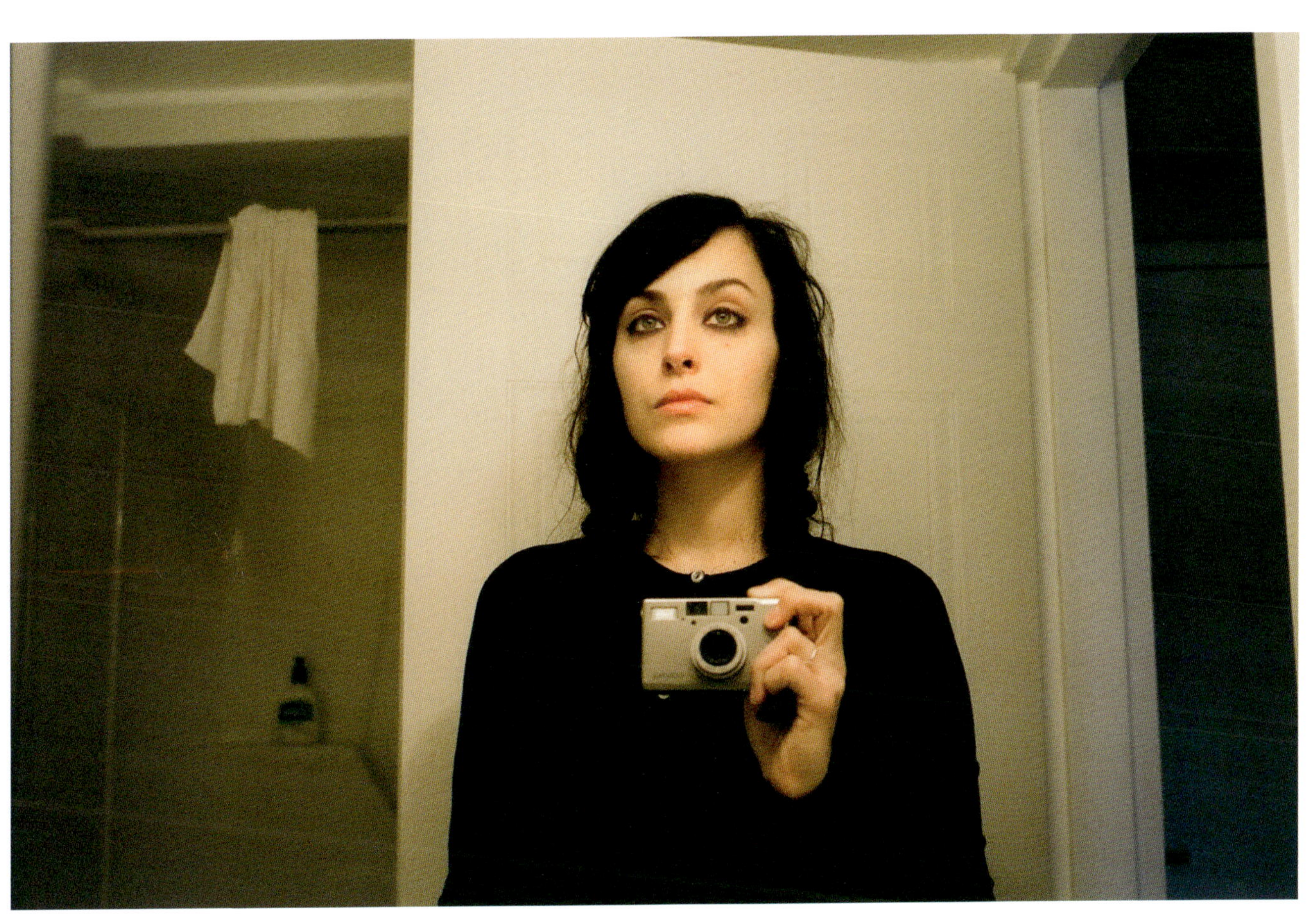

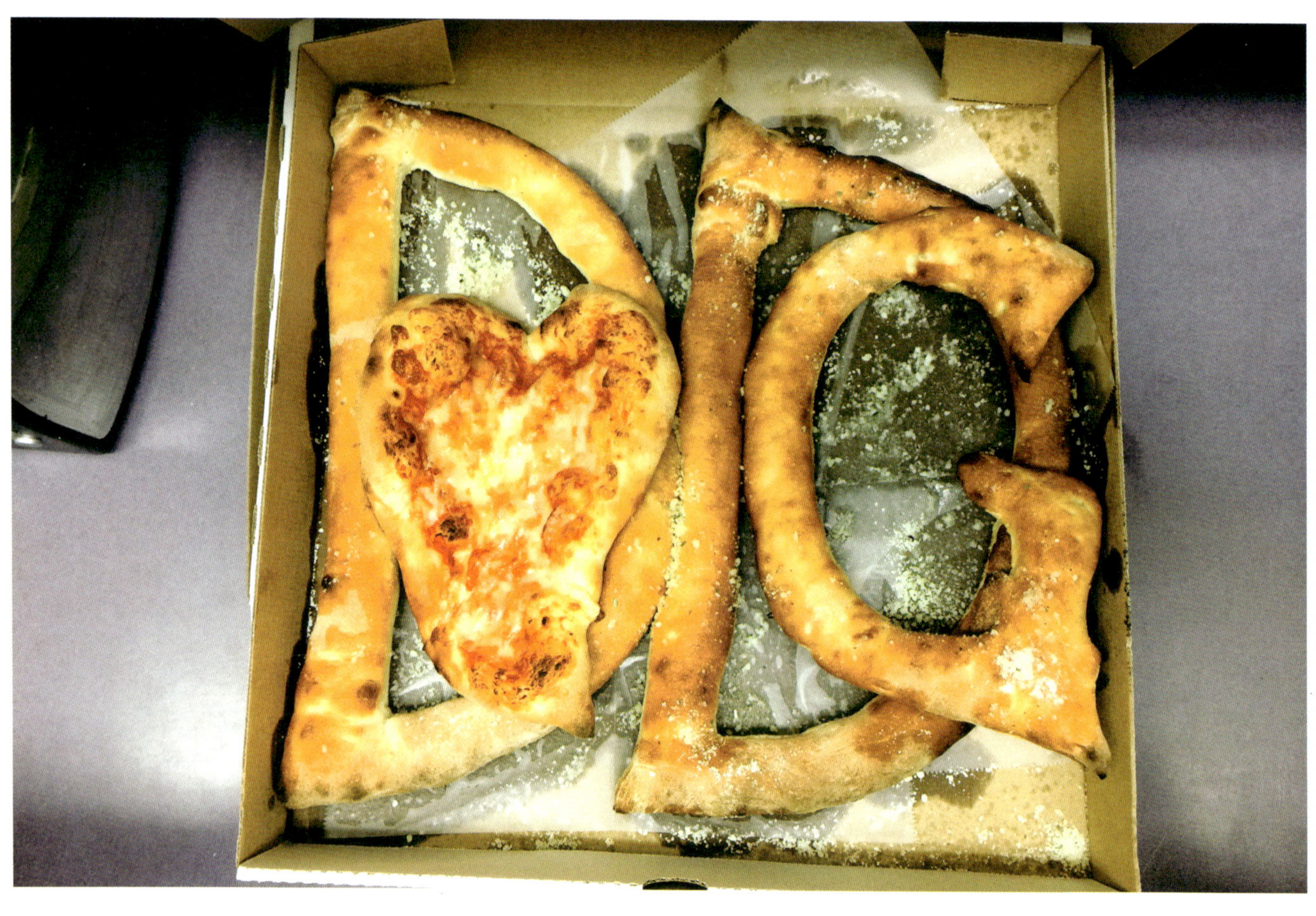

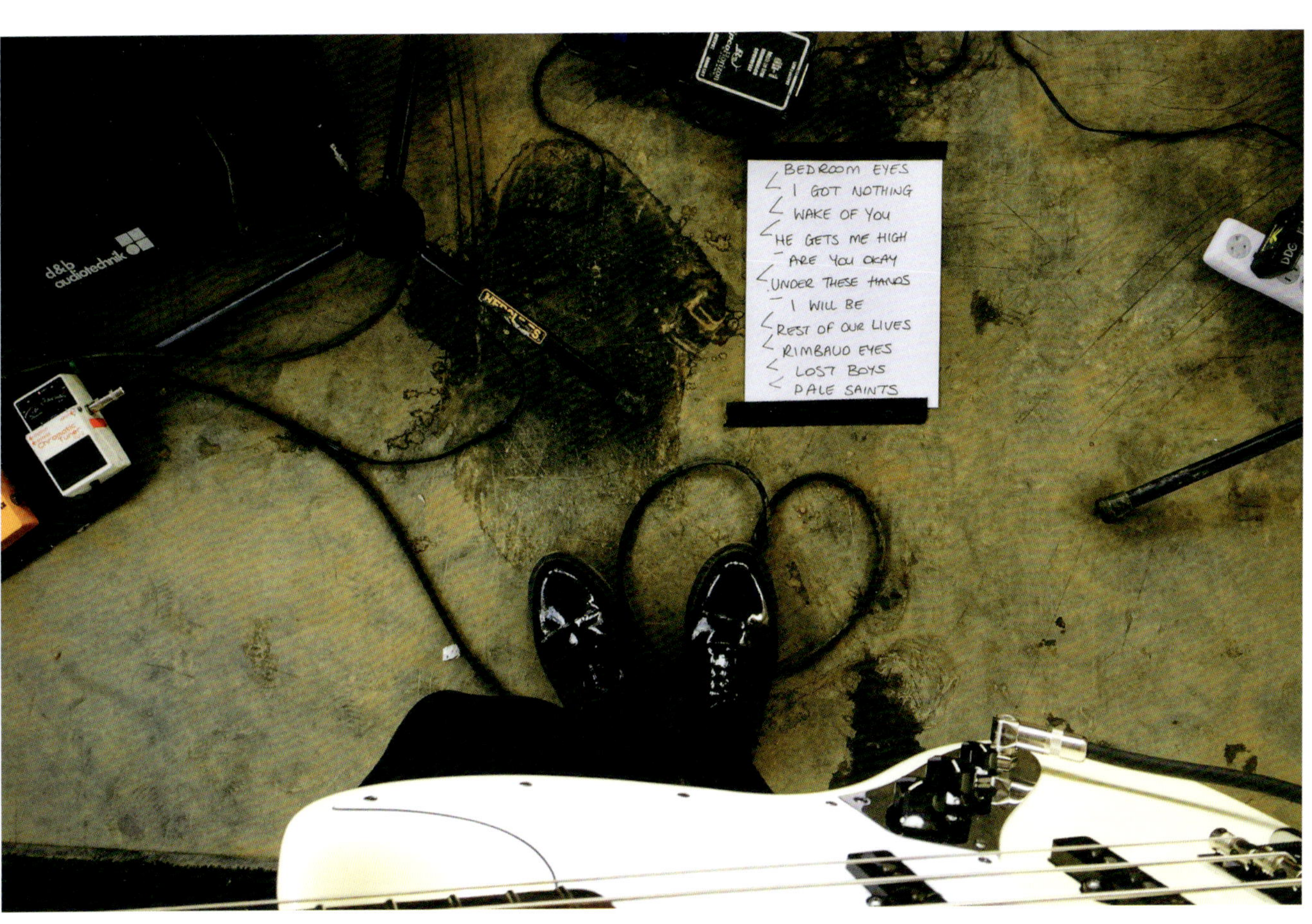
d&b audiotechnik
BEDROOM EYES
I GOT NOTHING
WAKE OF YOU
HE GETS ME HIGH
ARE YOU OKAY
UNDER THESE HANDS
I WILL BE
REST OF OUR LIVES
RIMBAUD EYES
LOST BOYS
PALE SAINTS

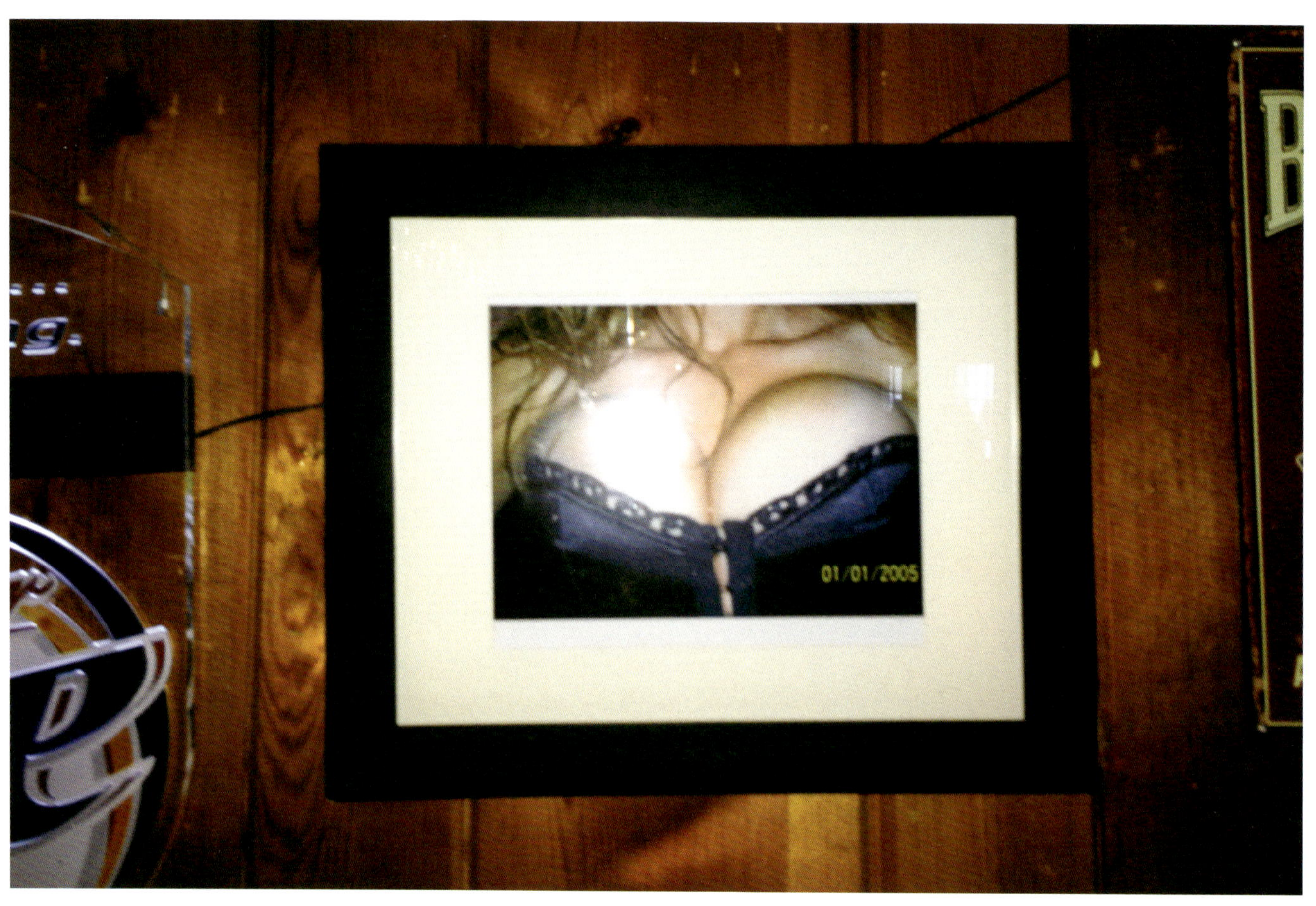
01/01/2005

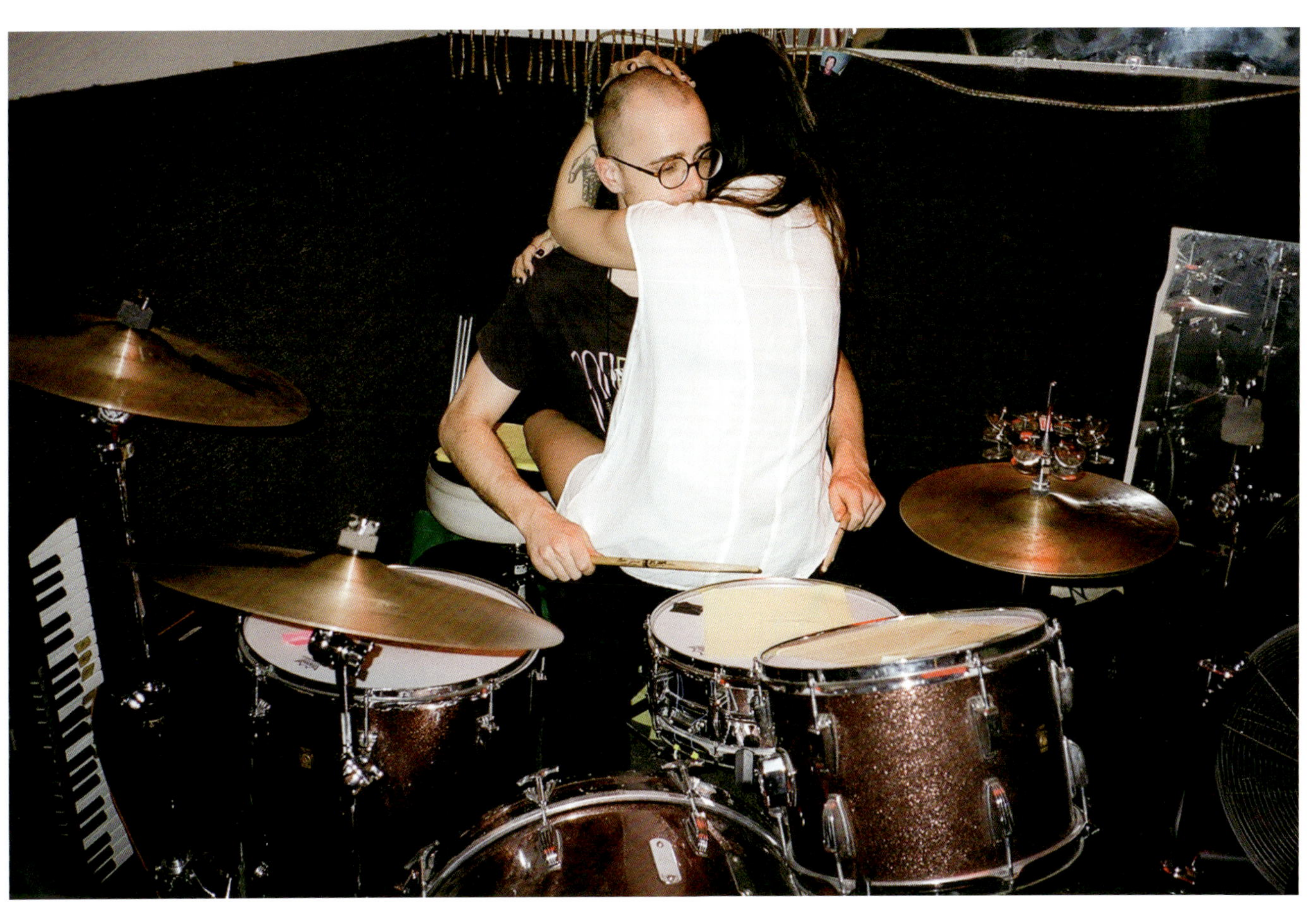

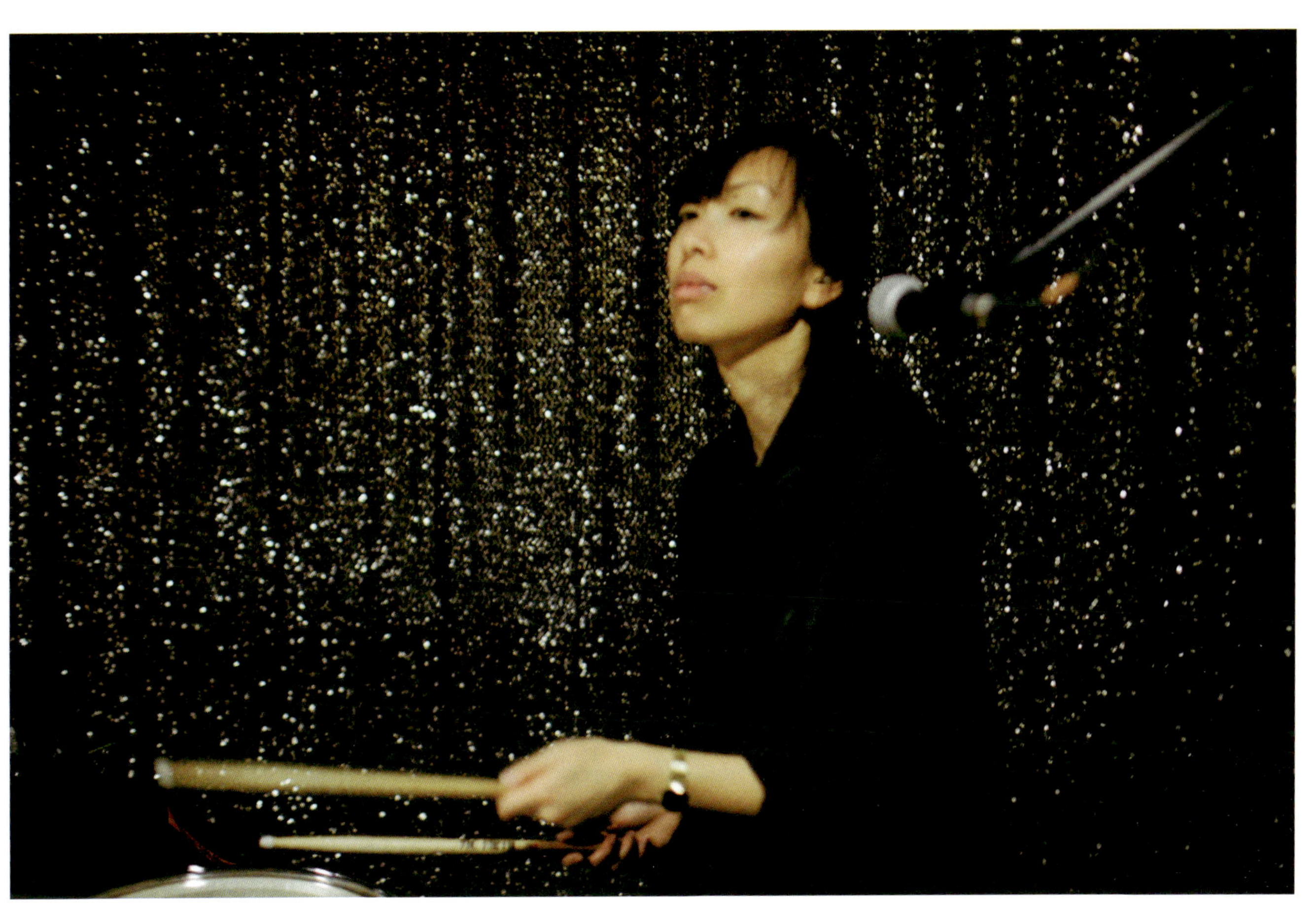

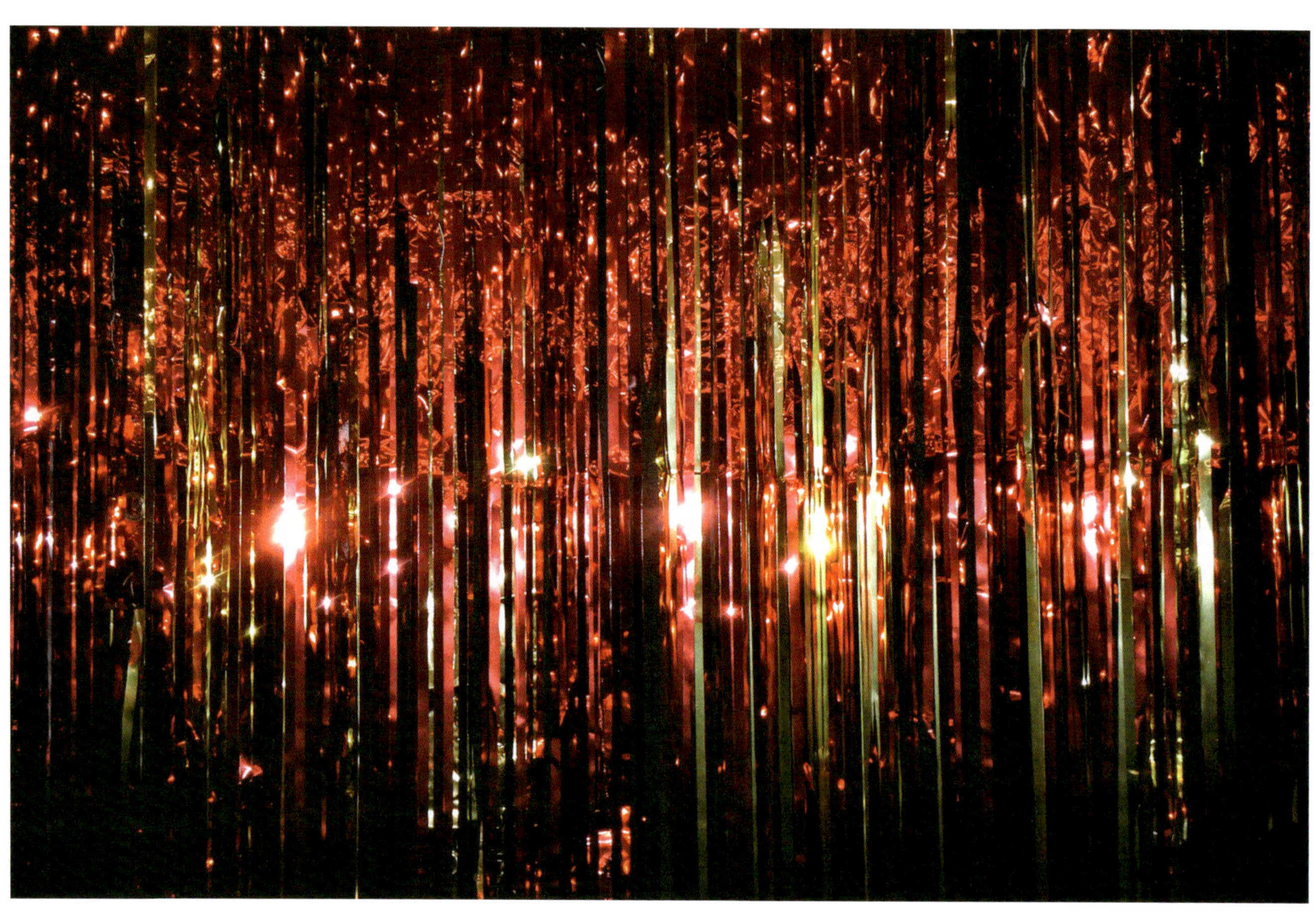

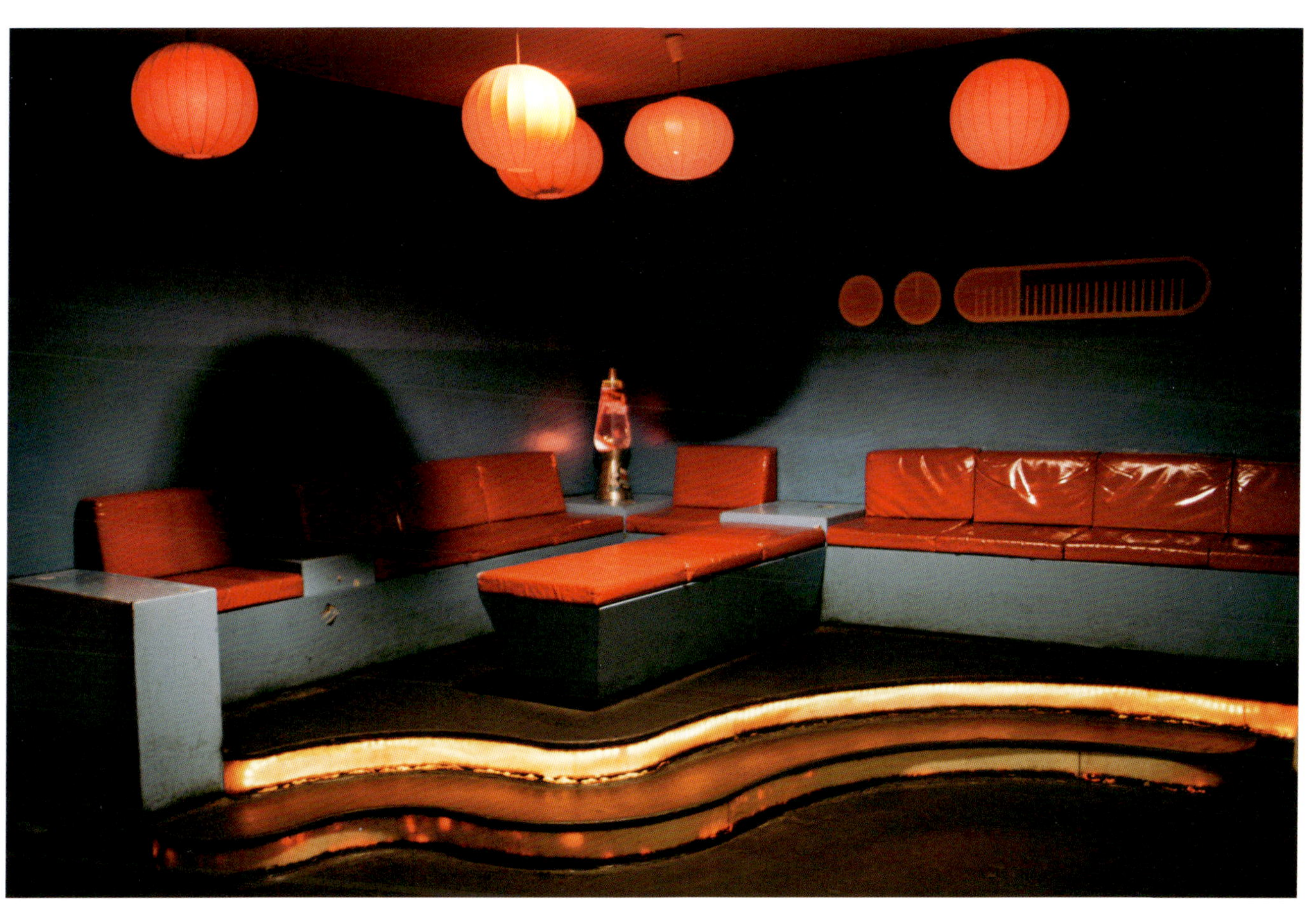

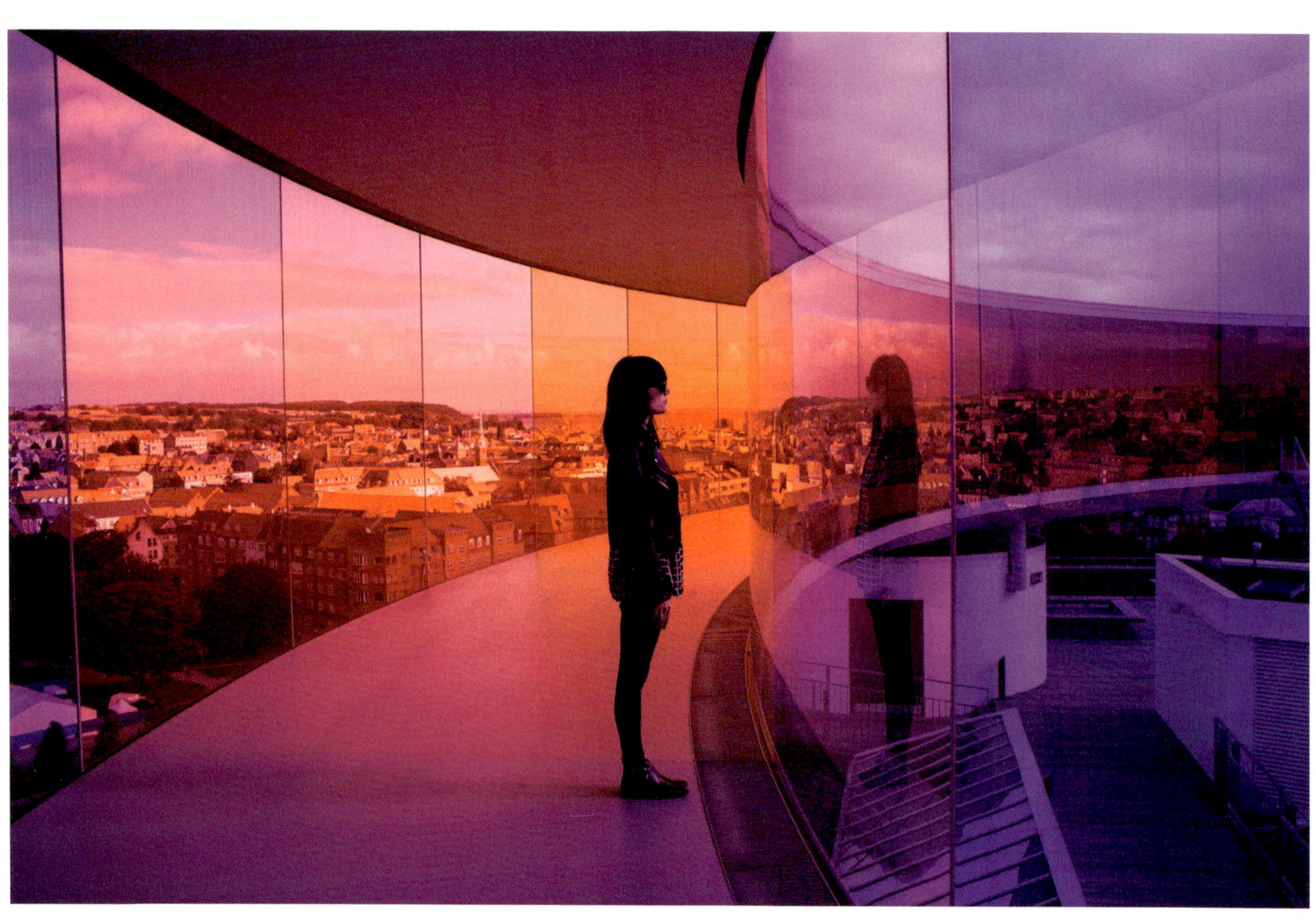

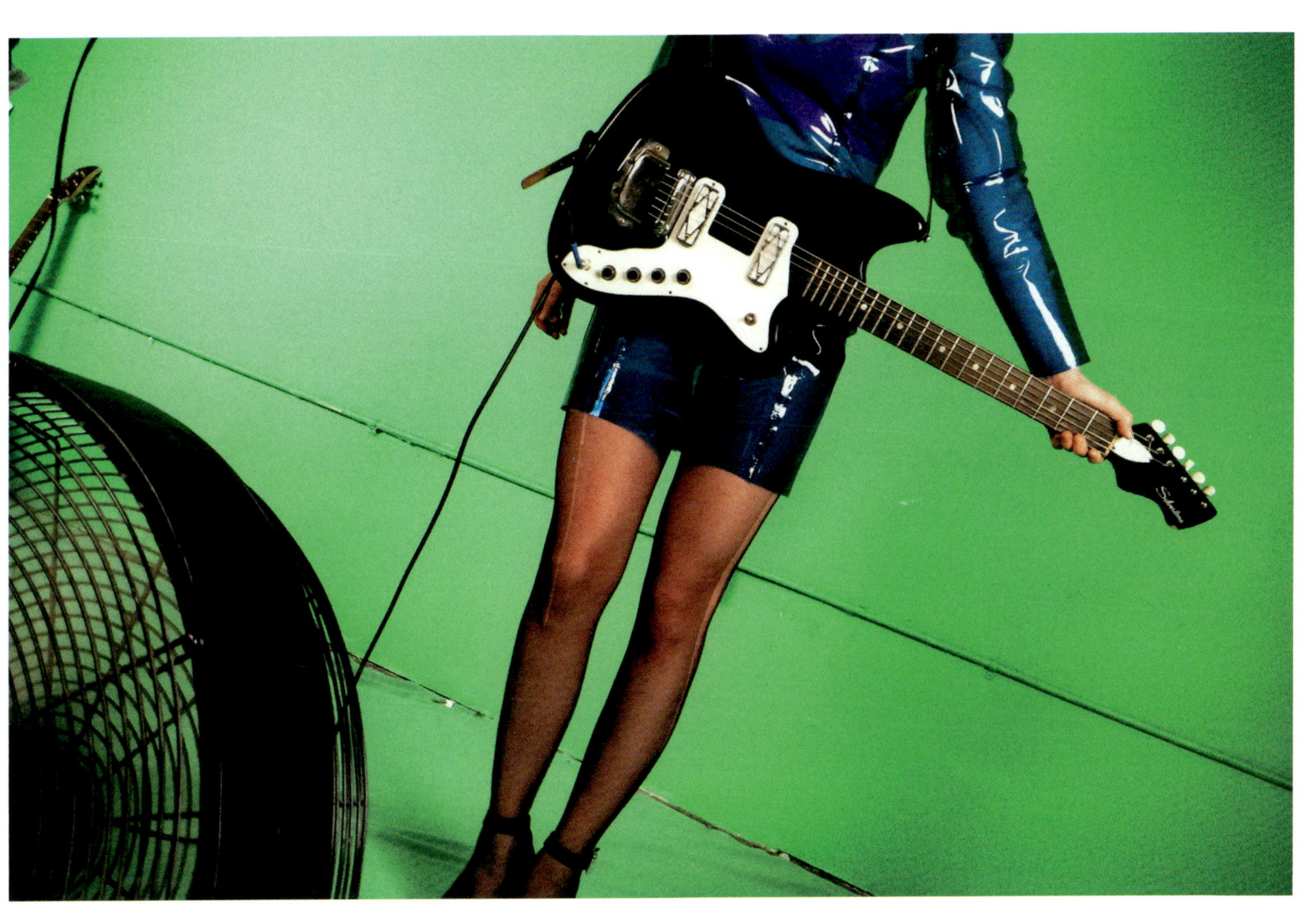

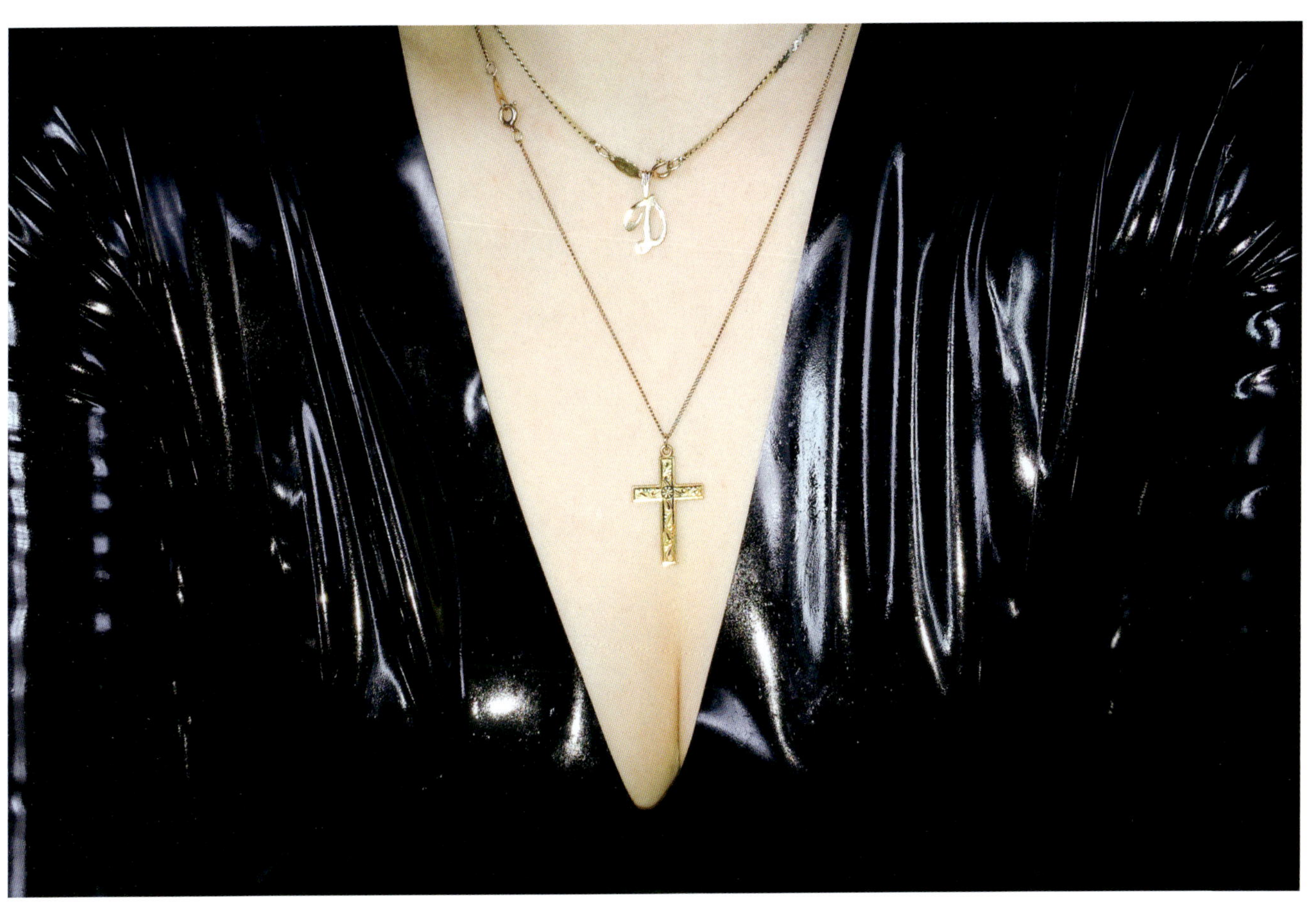

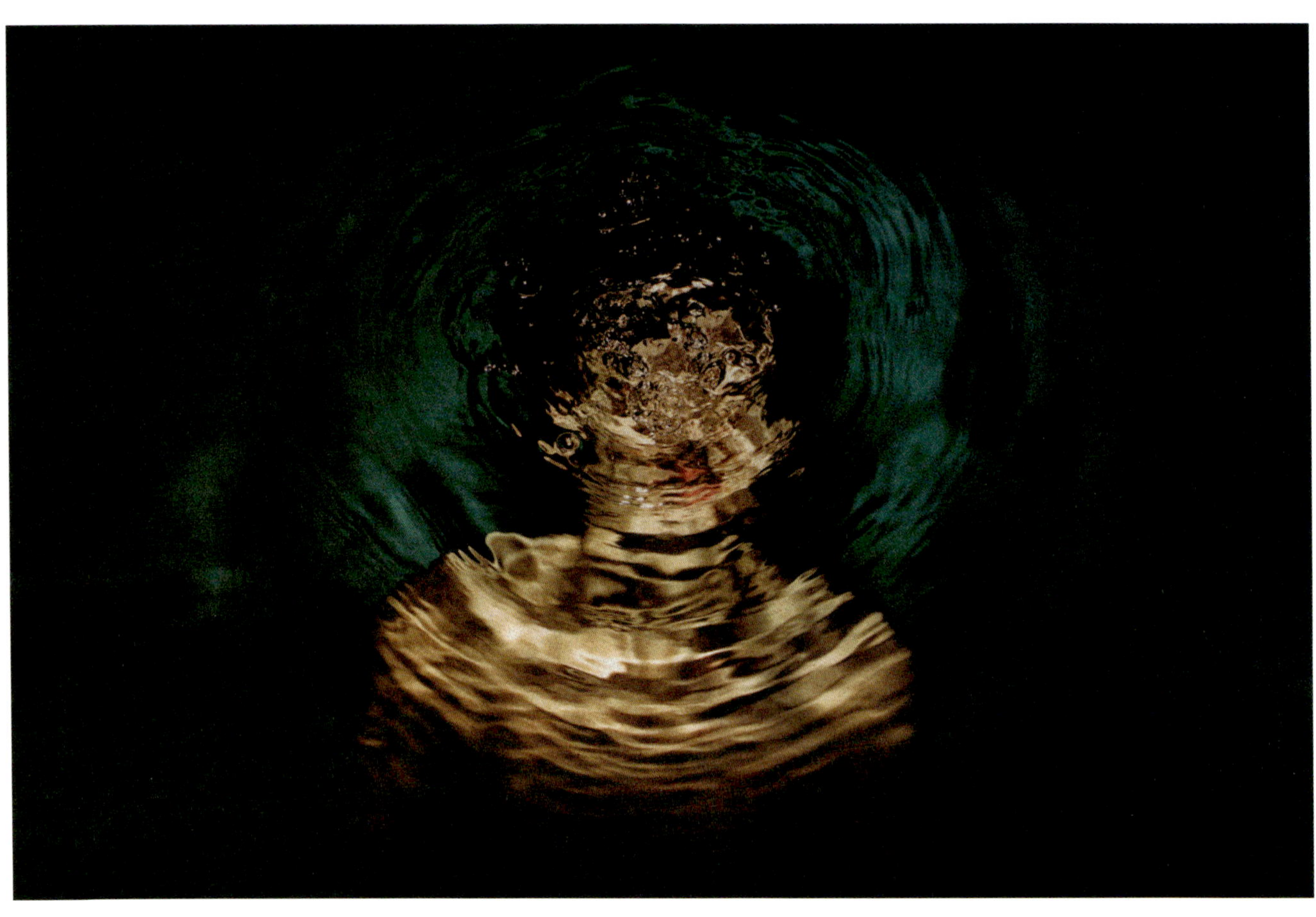

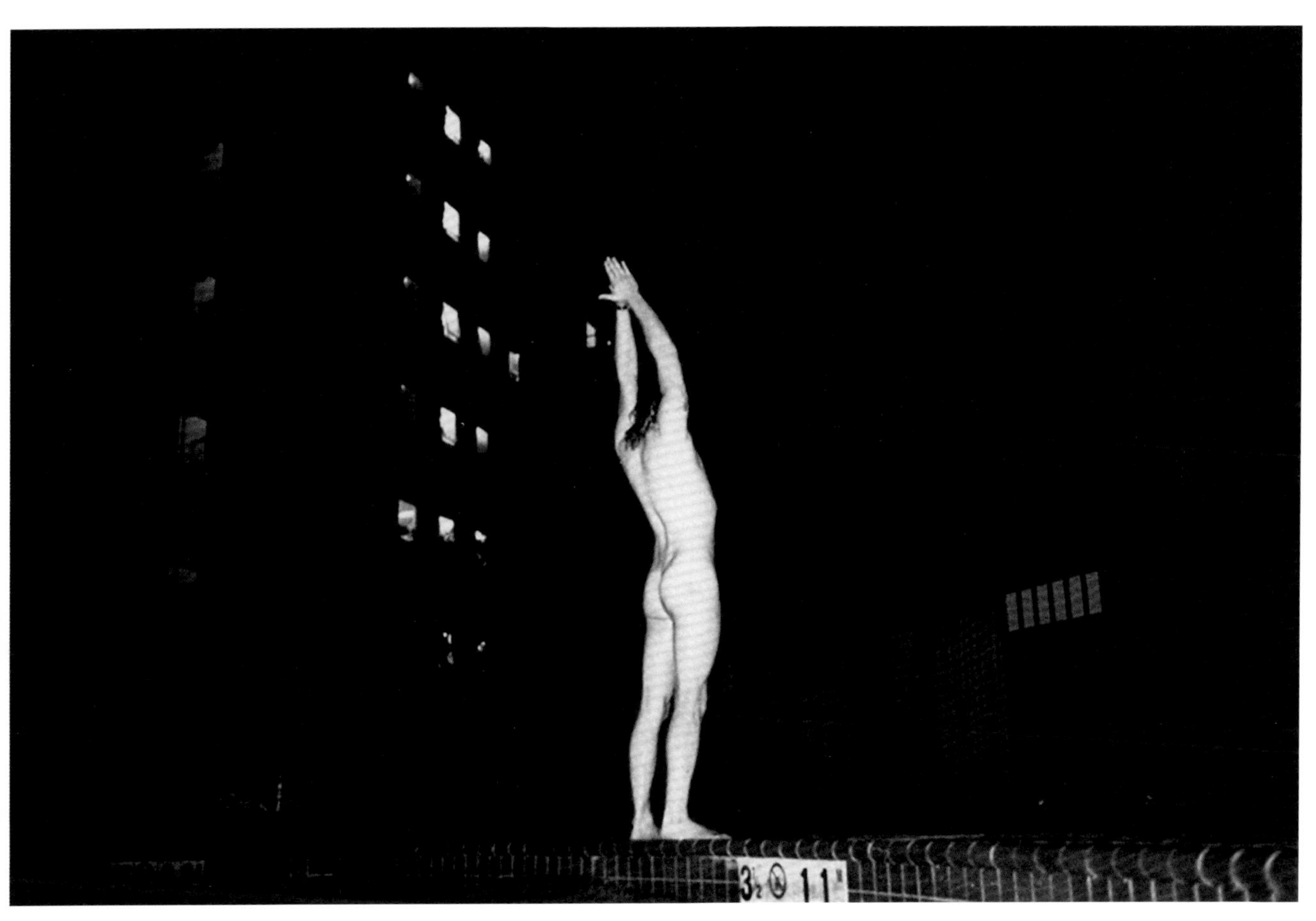
3½
11

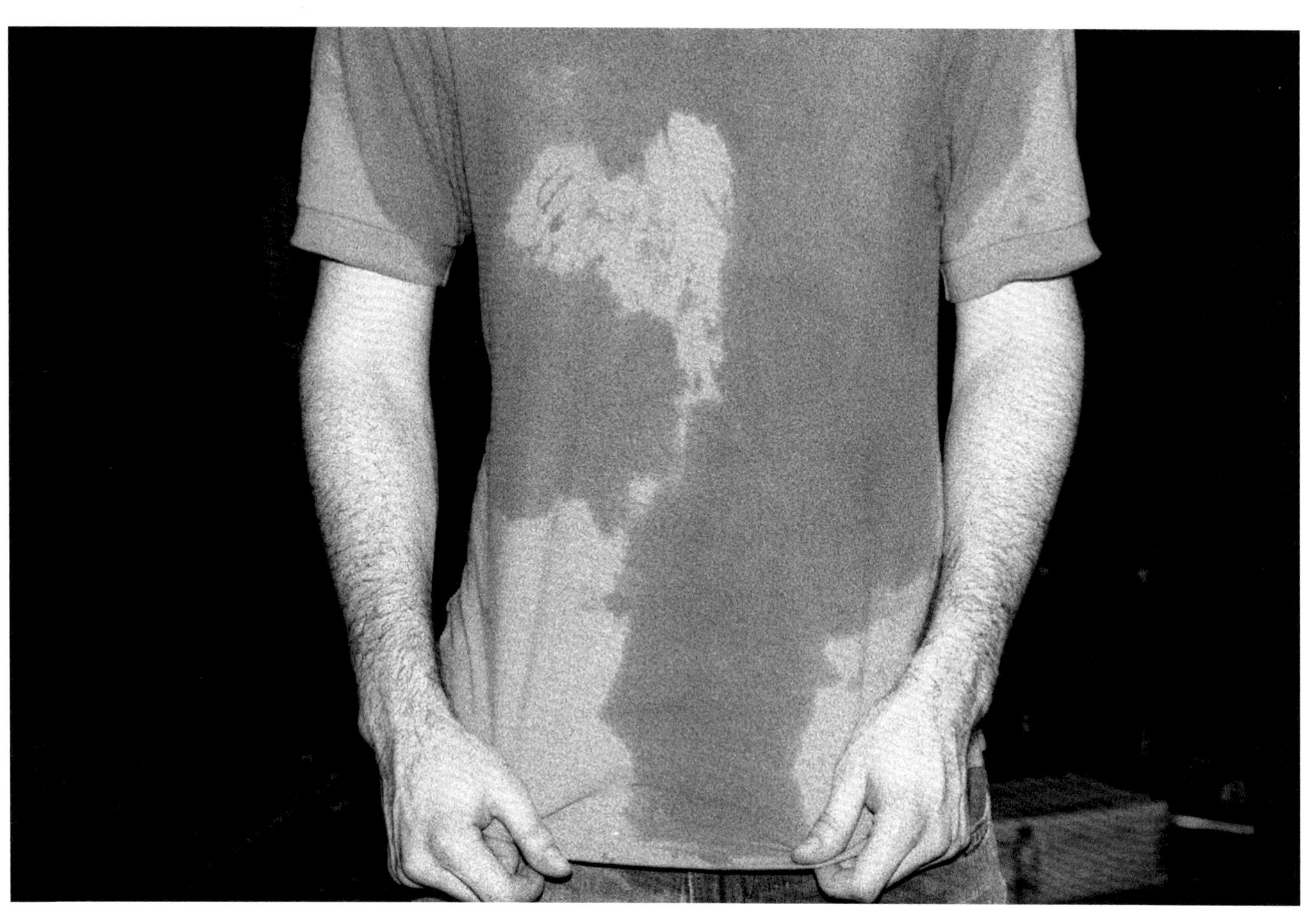

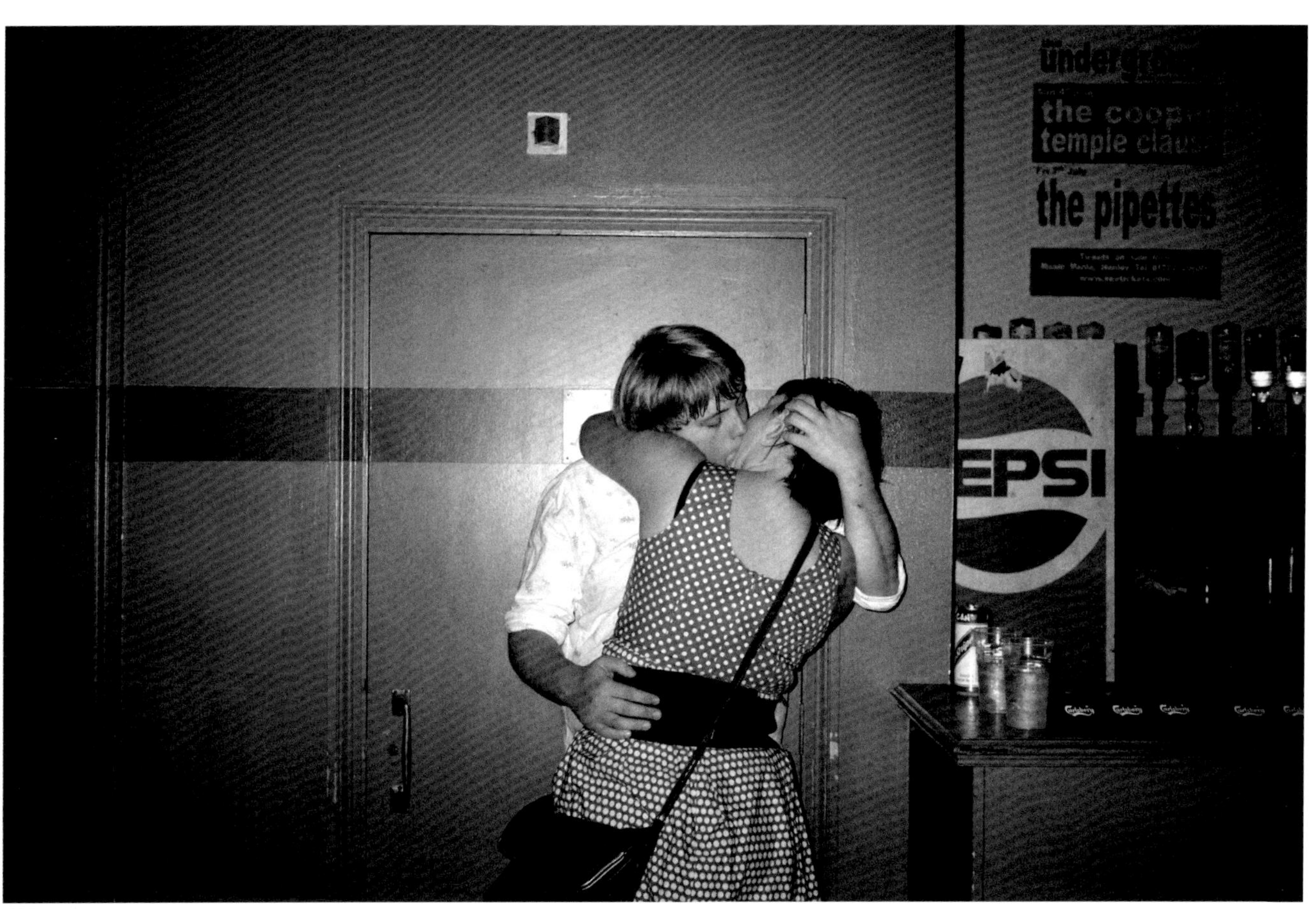
the pipettes

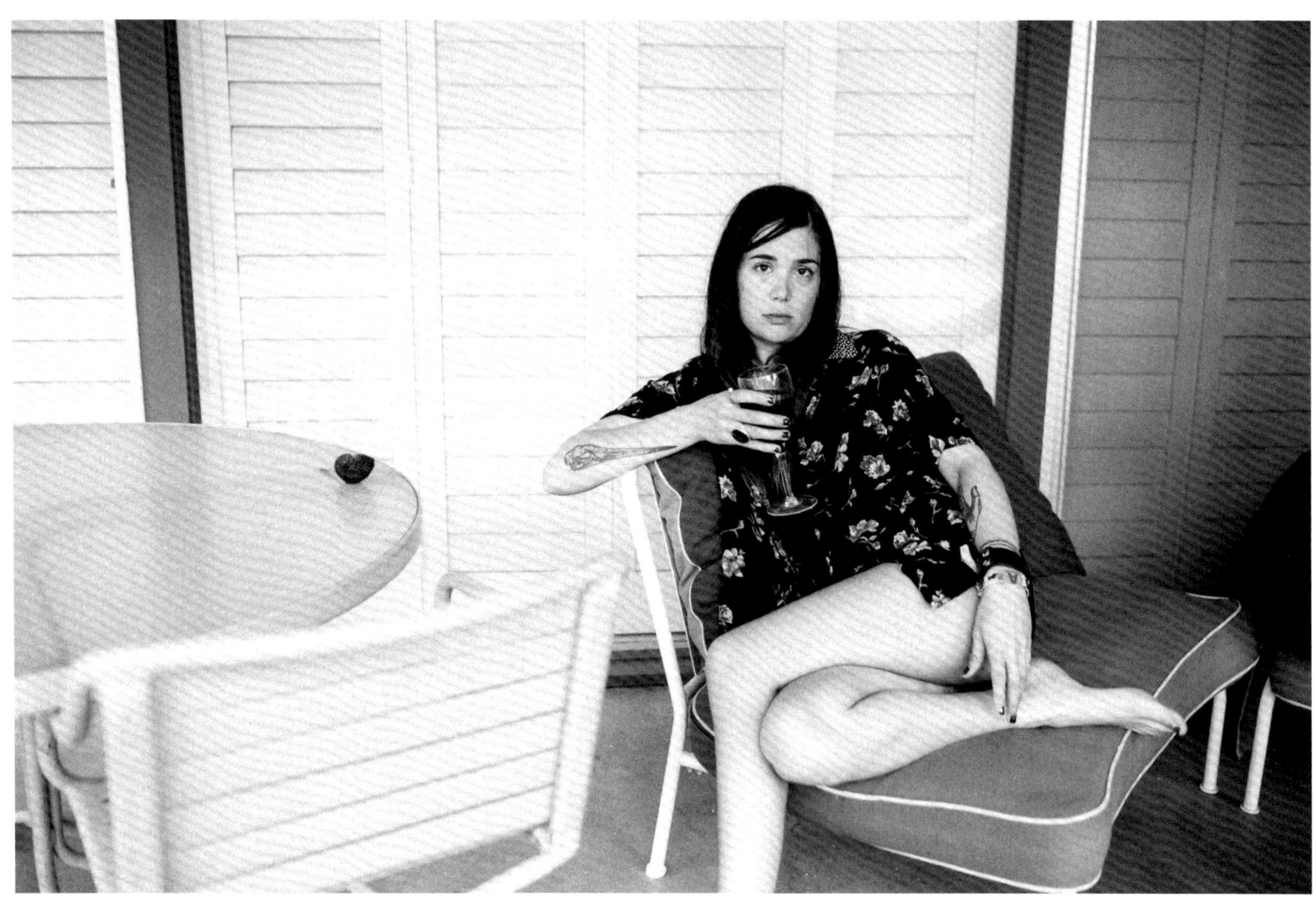

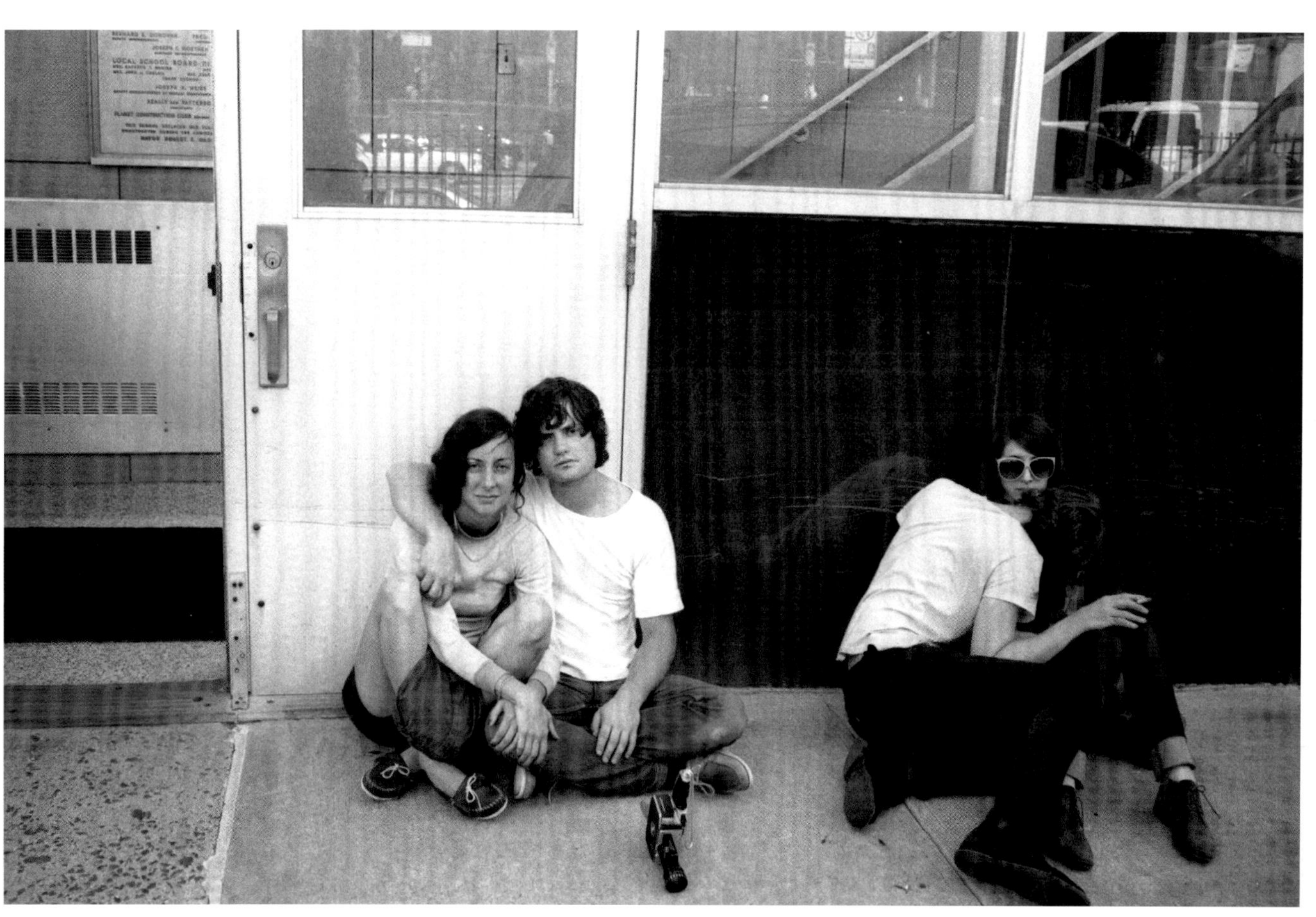

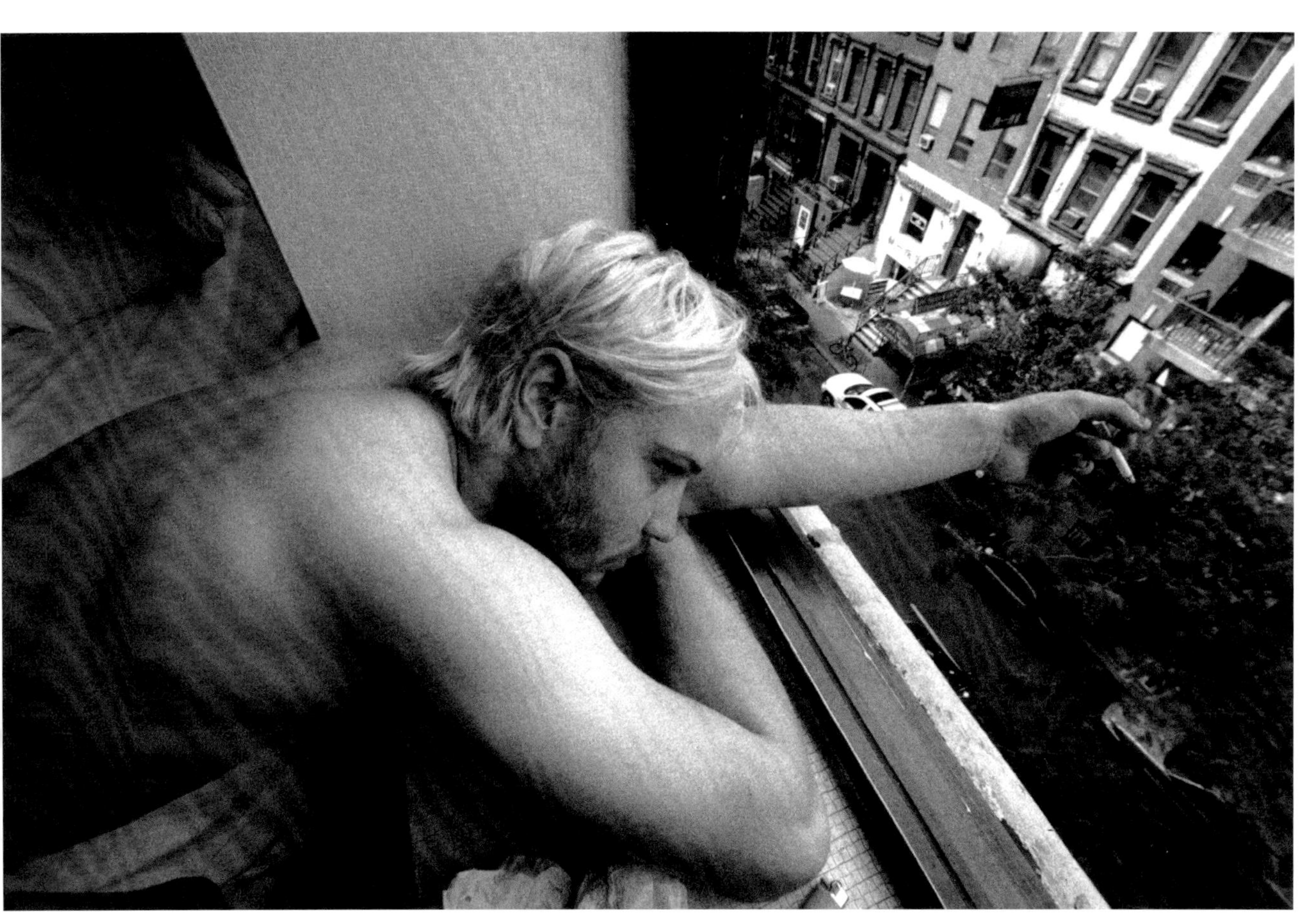

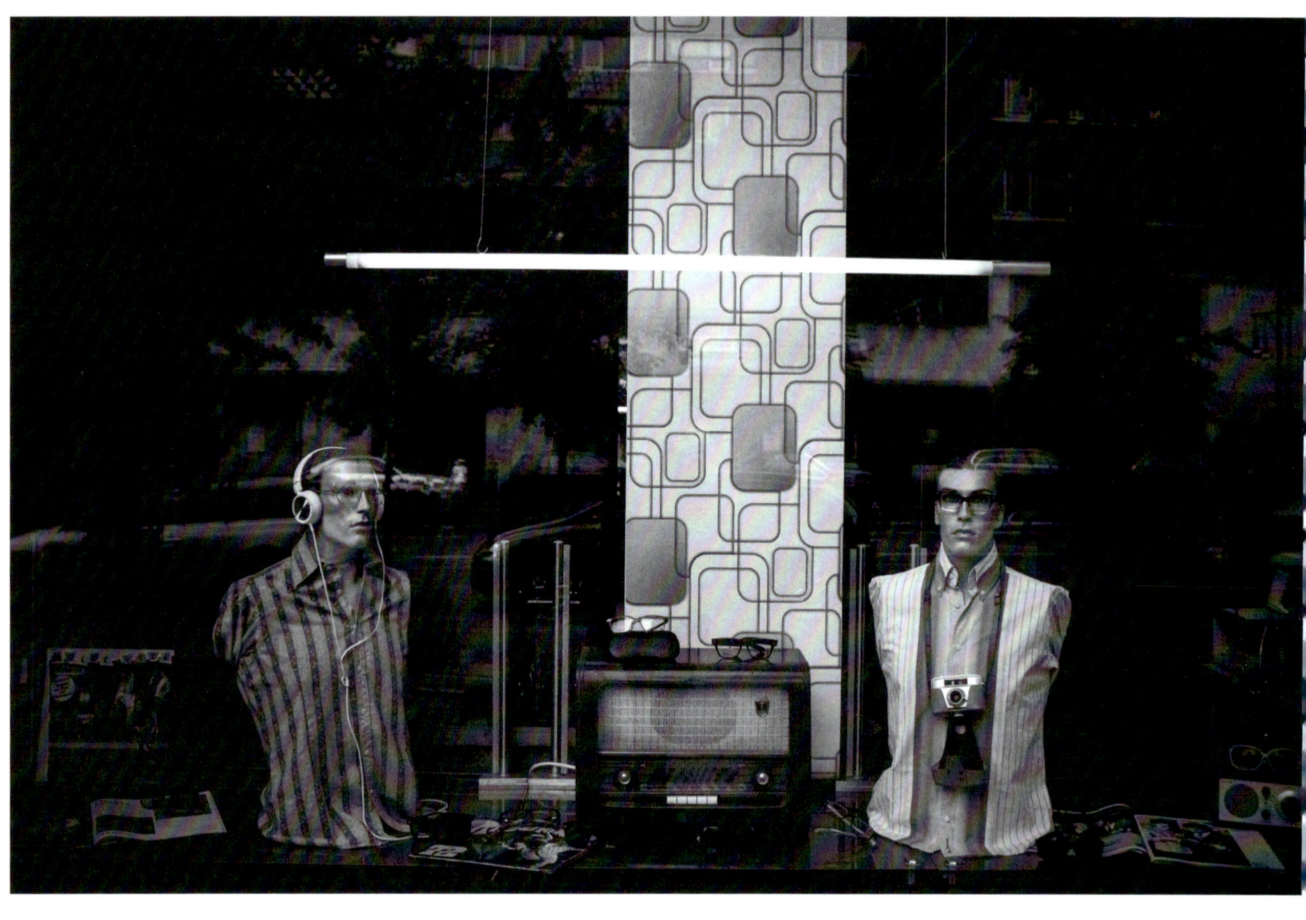

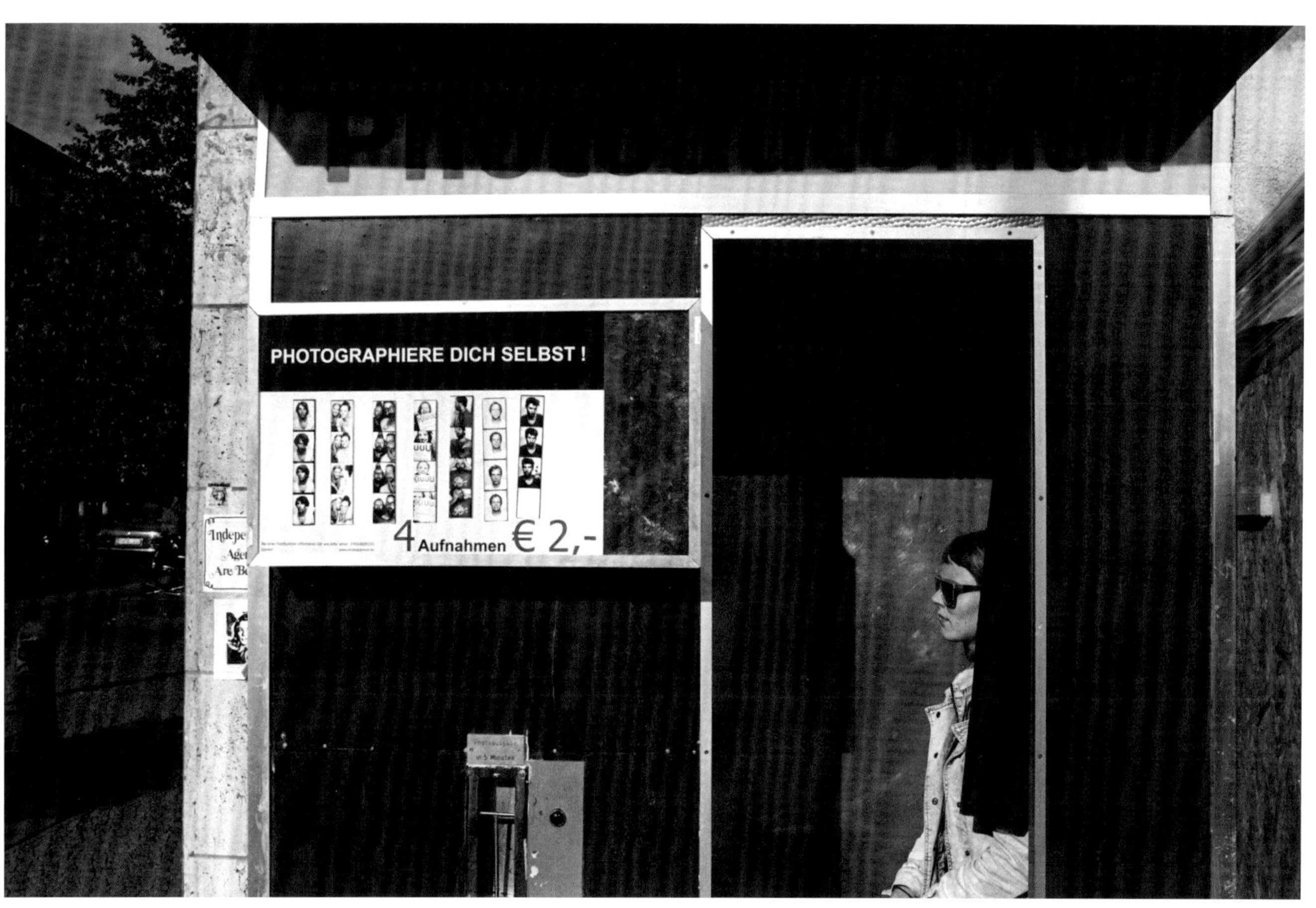
PHOTOGRAPHIERE DICH SELBST !
4 Aufnahmen € 2,-

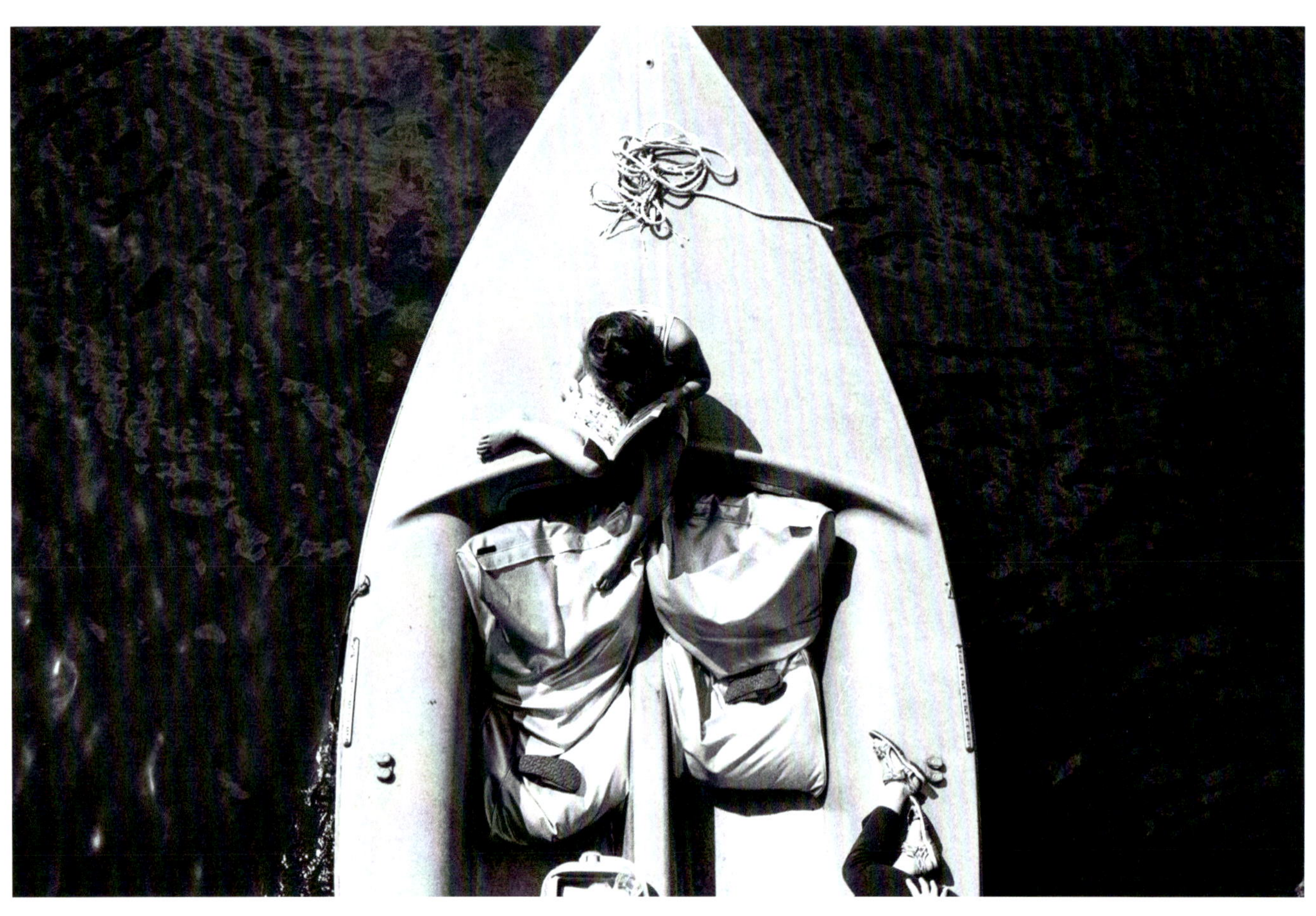

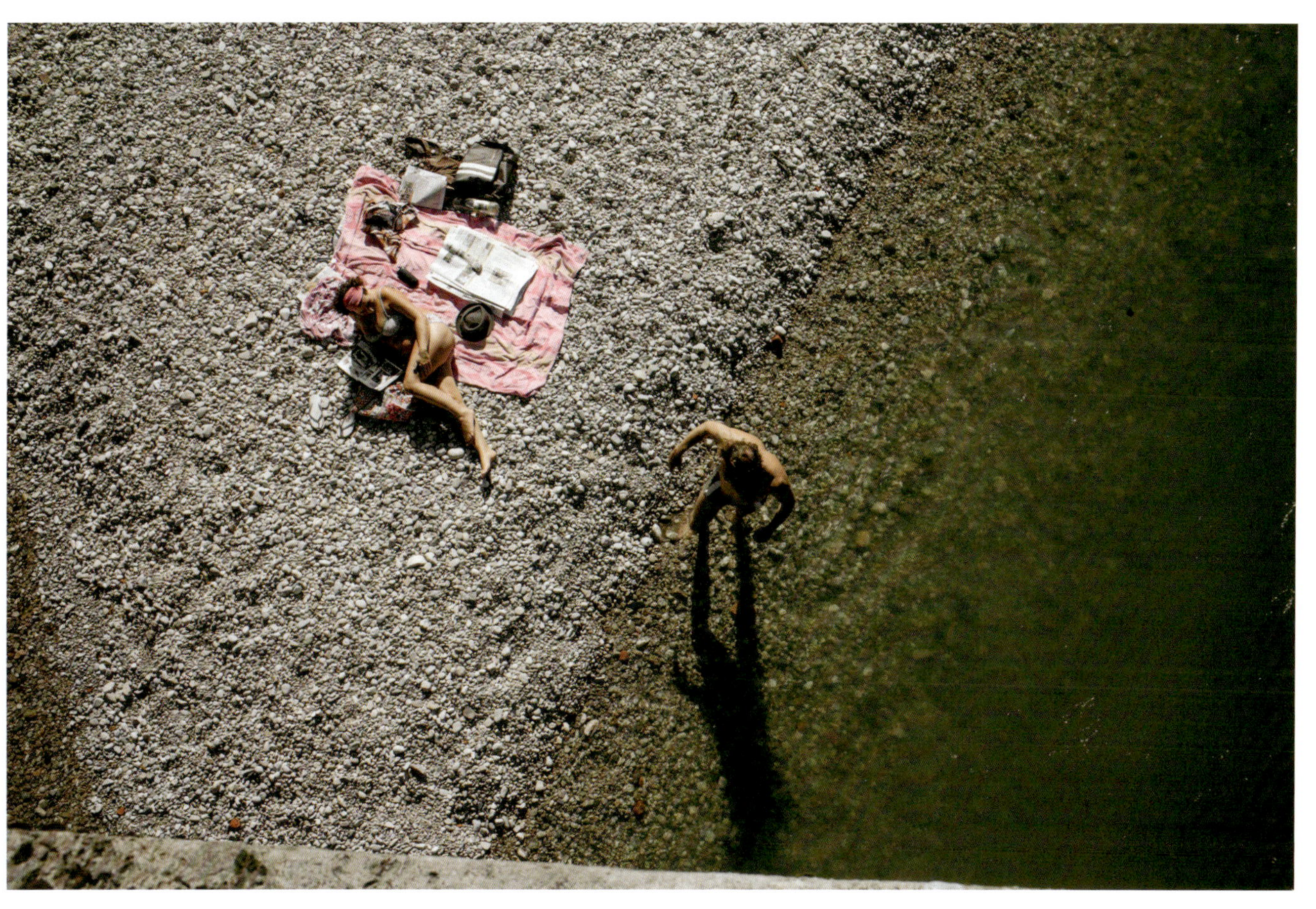

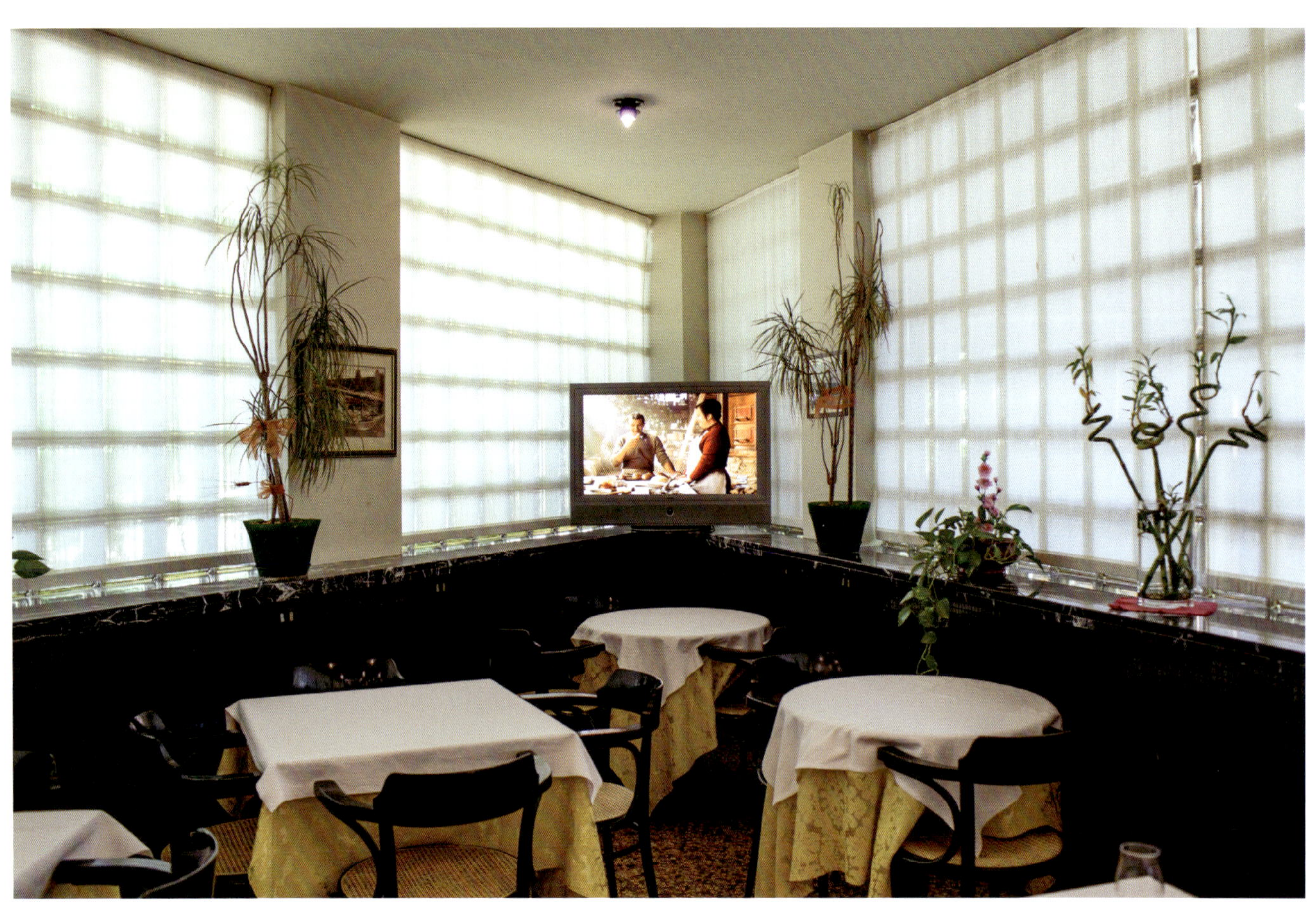

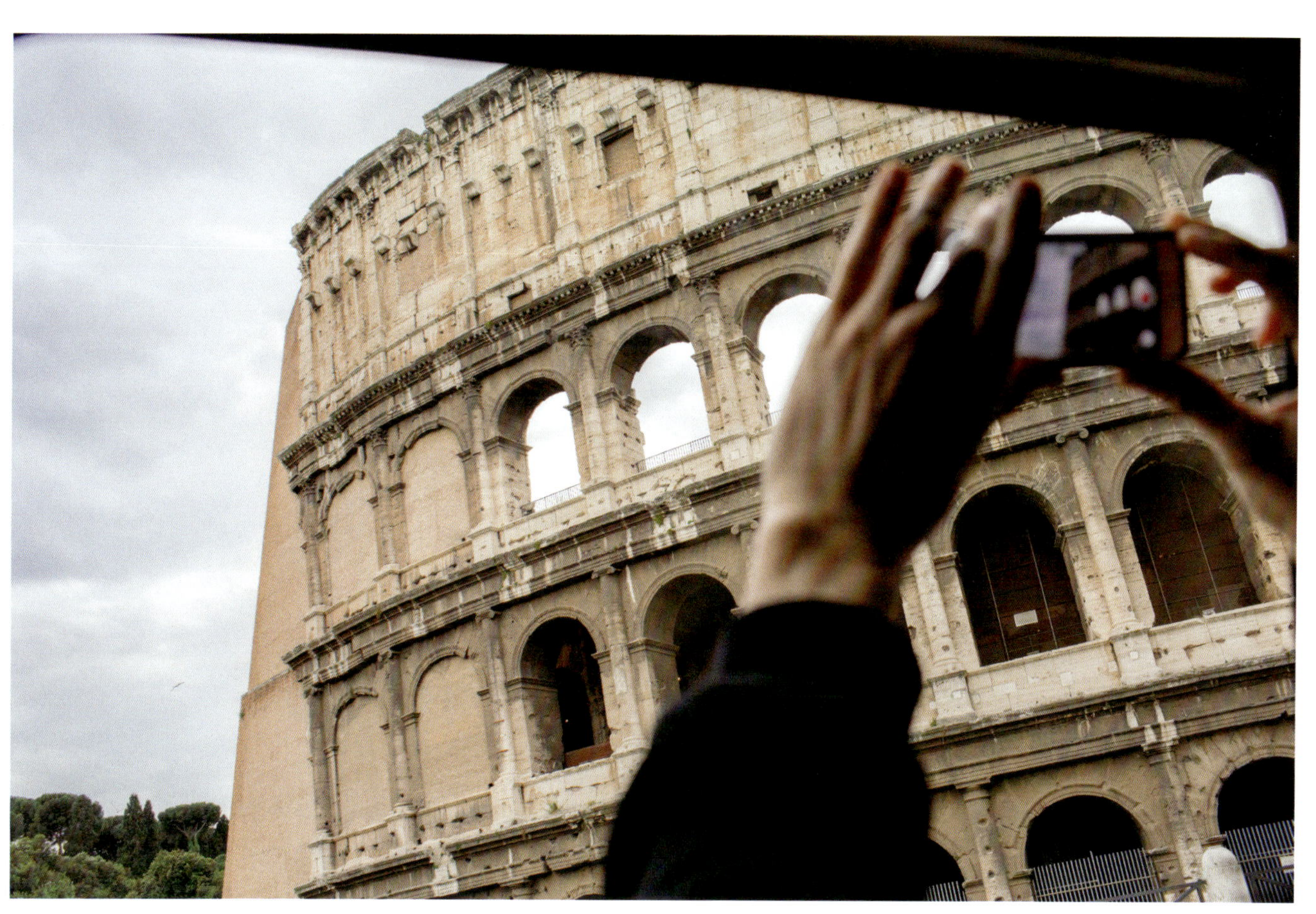

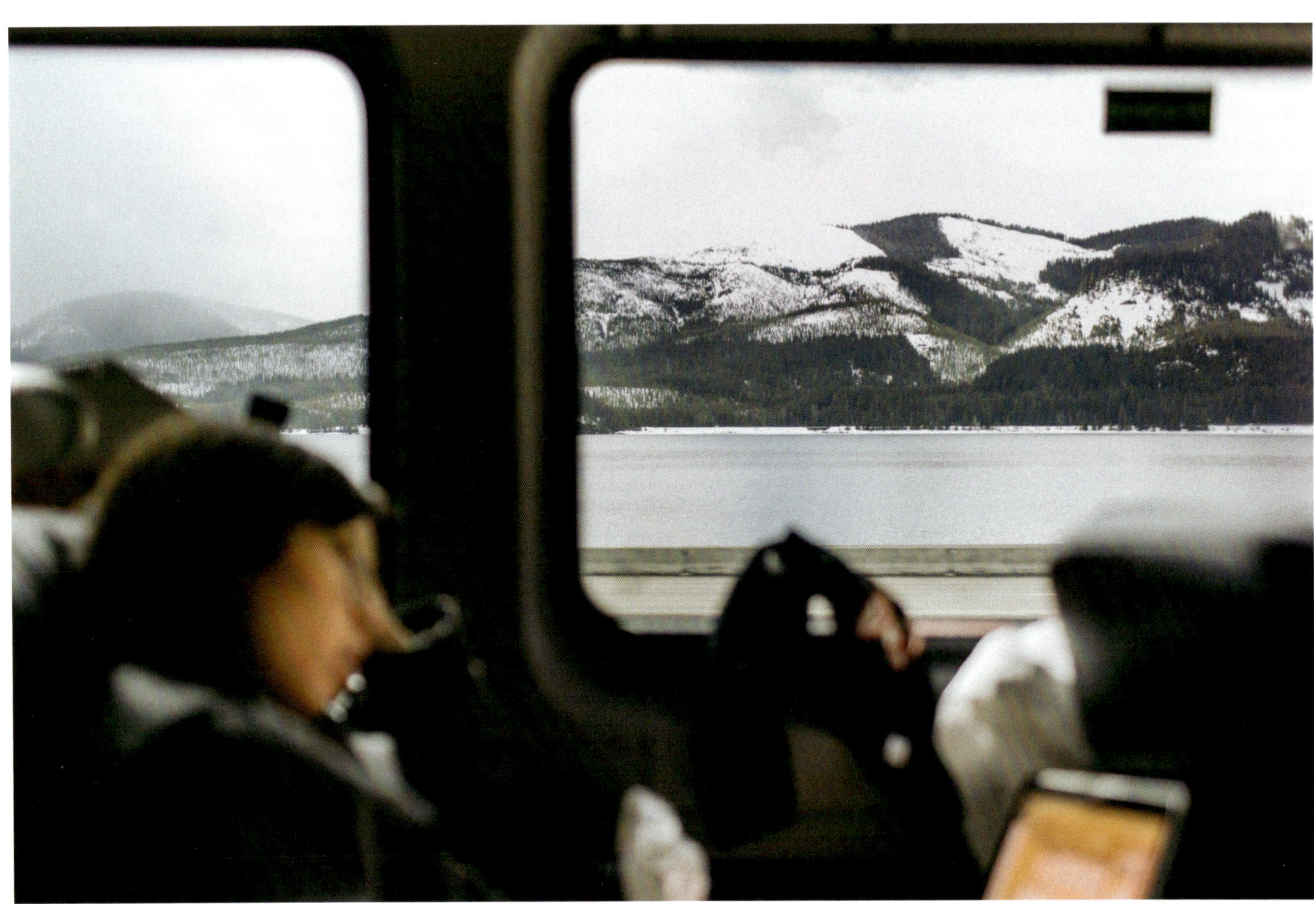

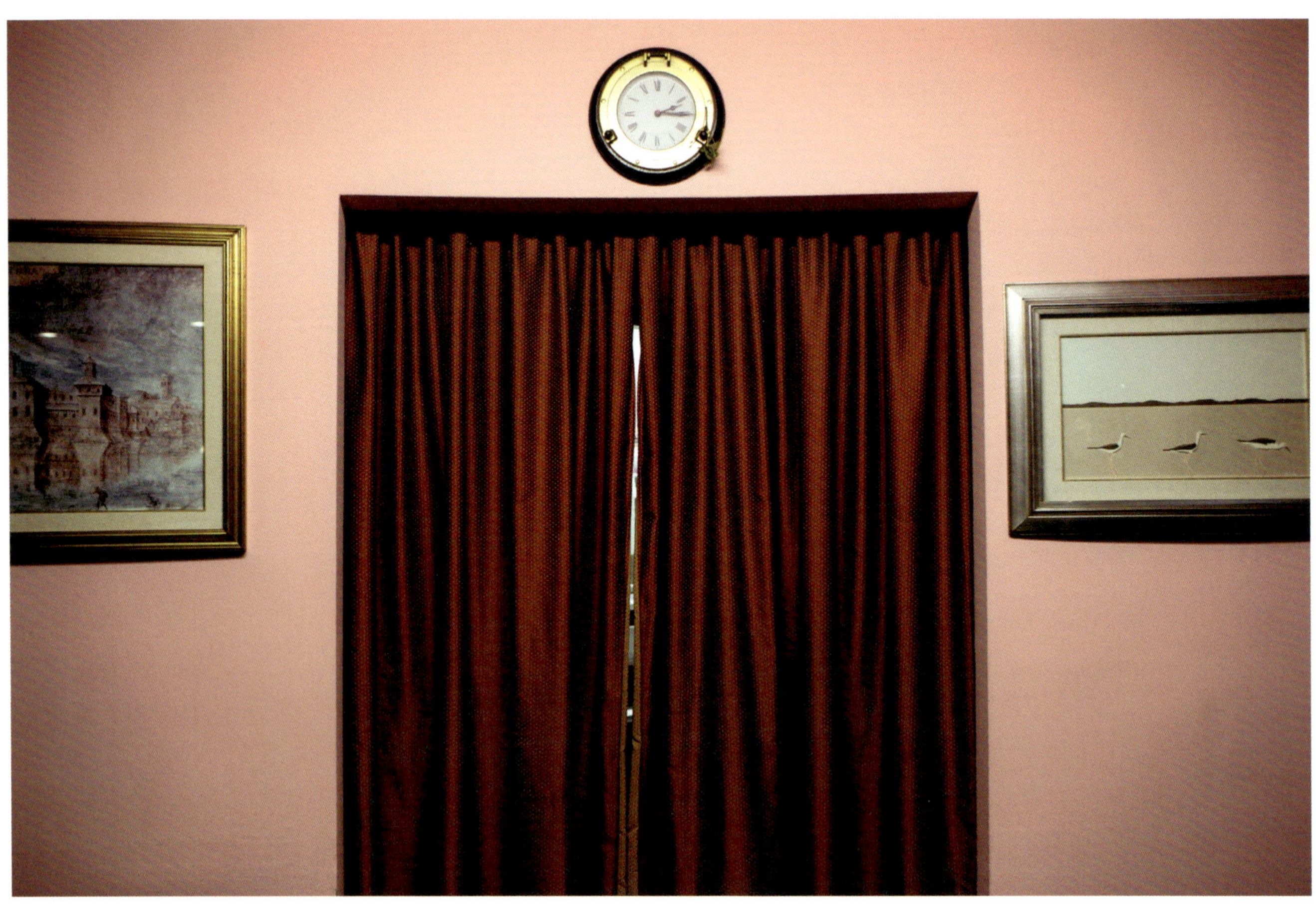

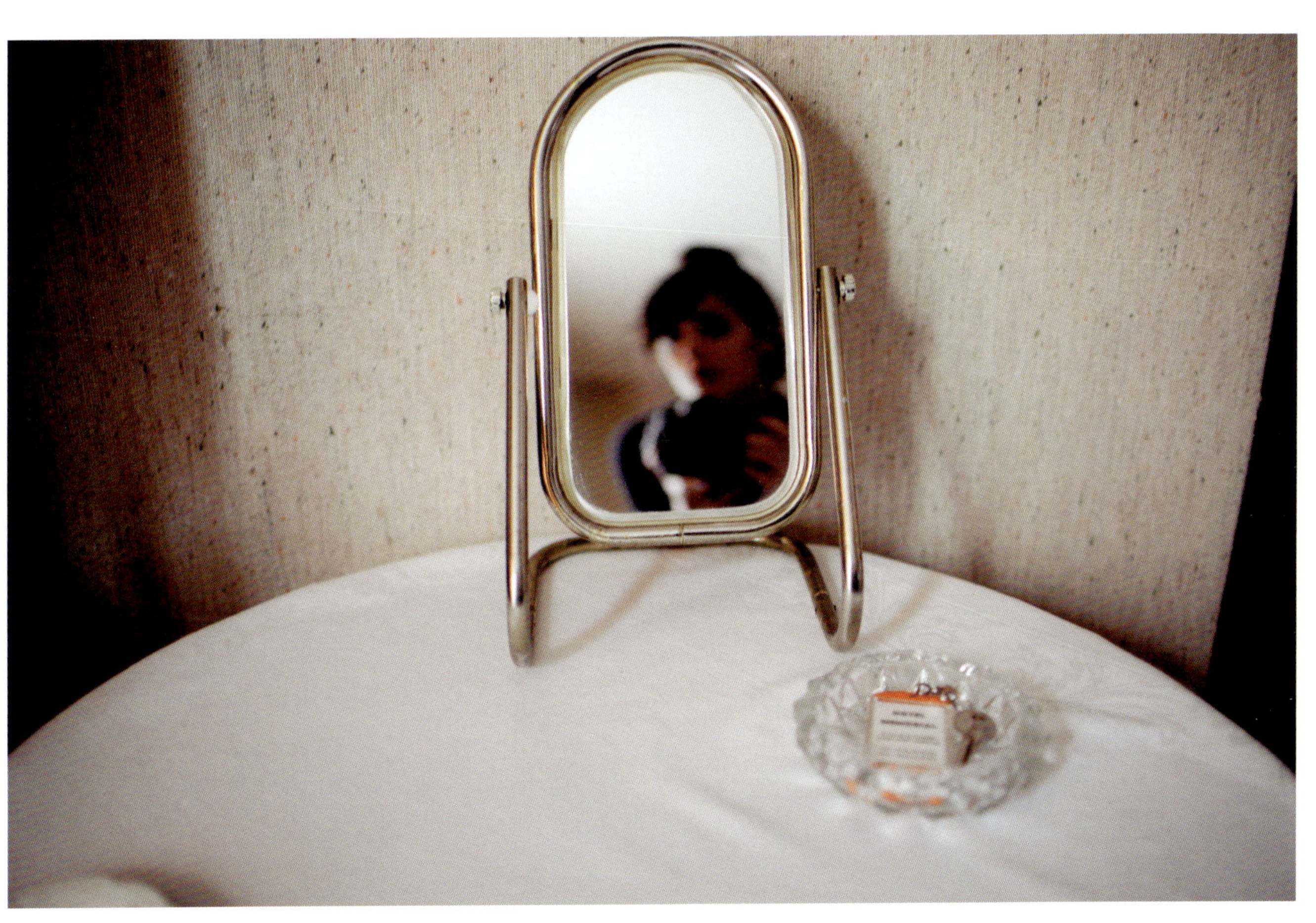

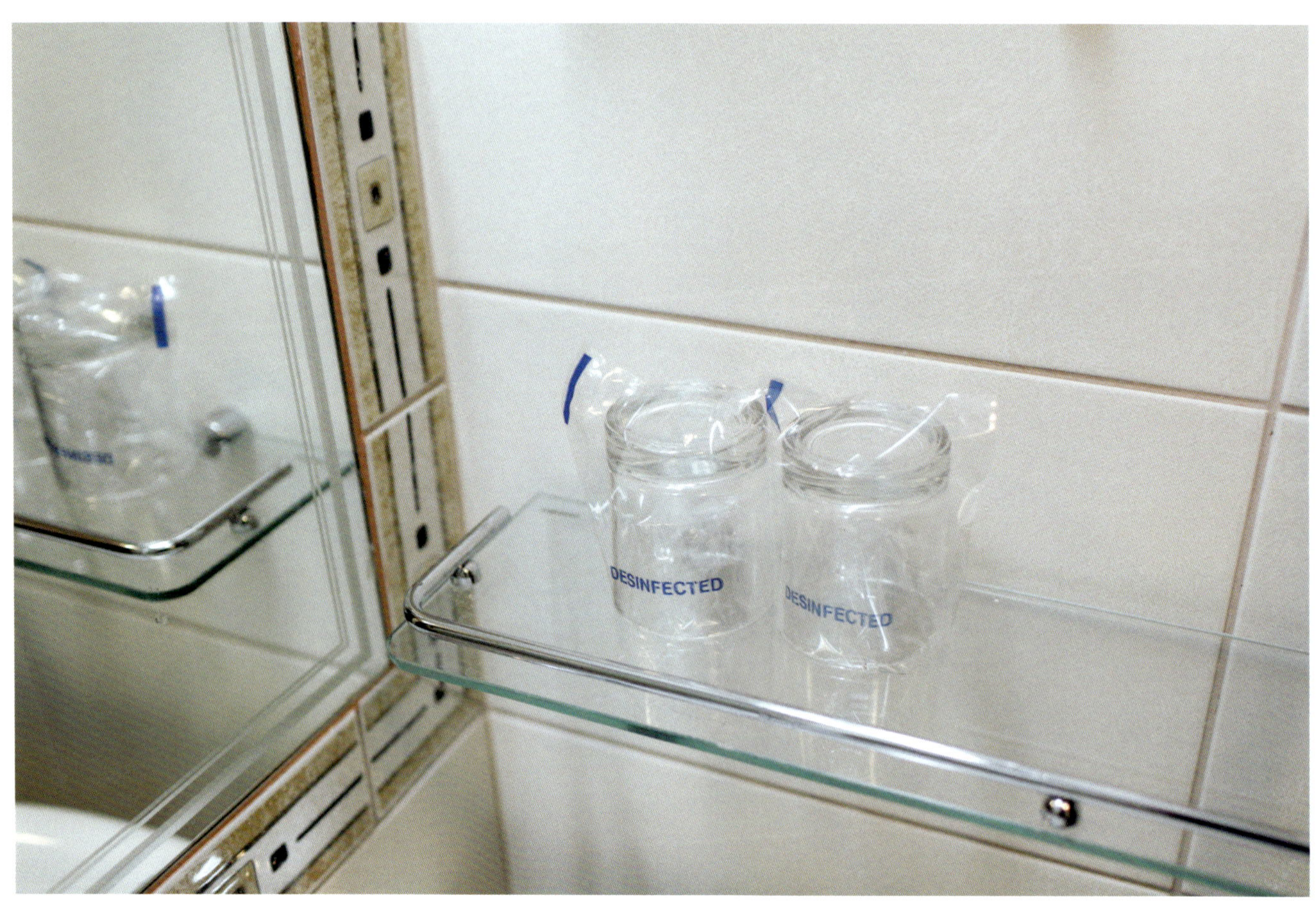
DESINFECTED
DESINFECTED

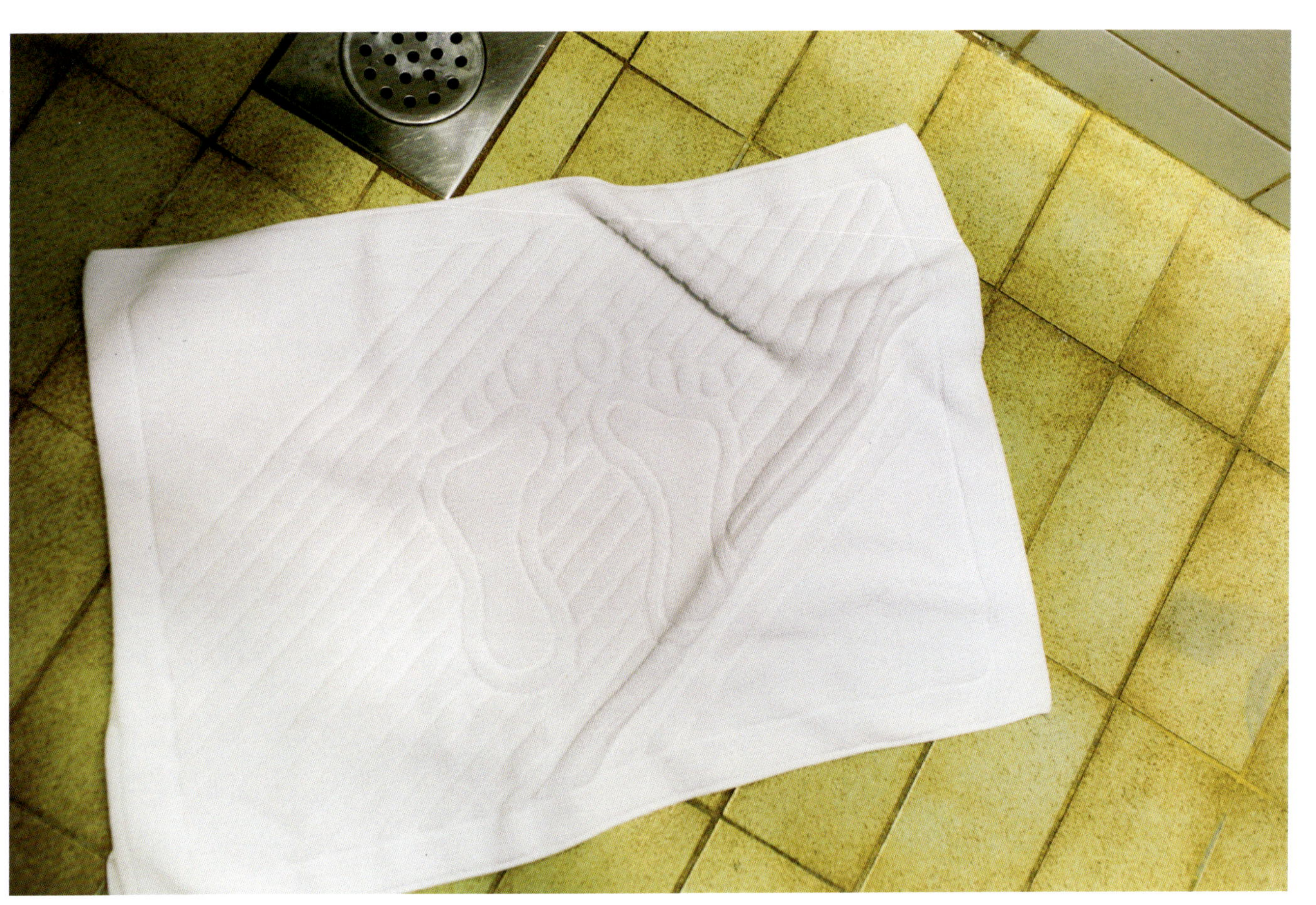

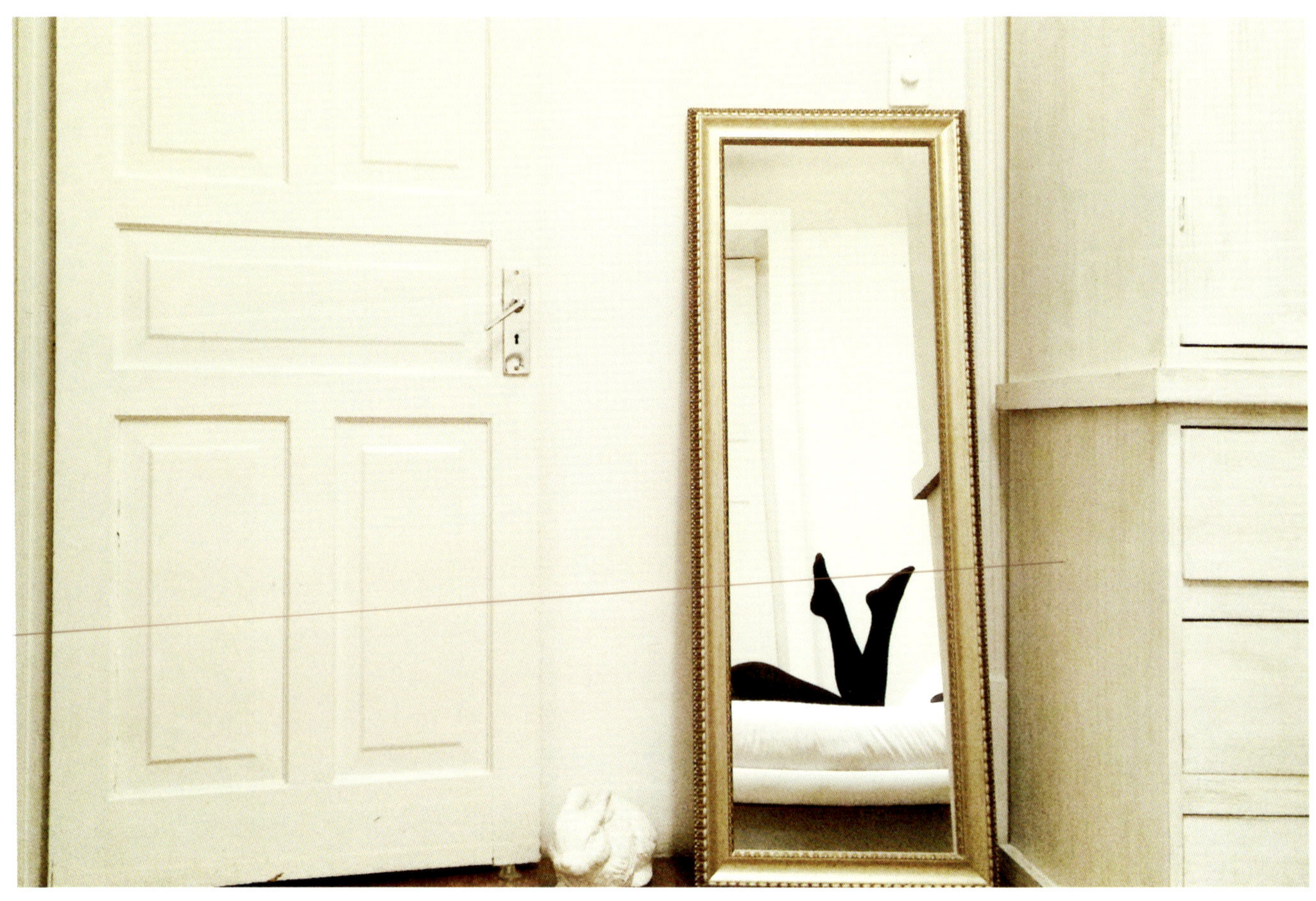

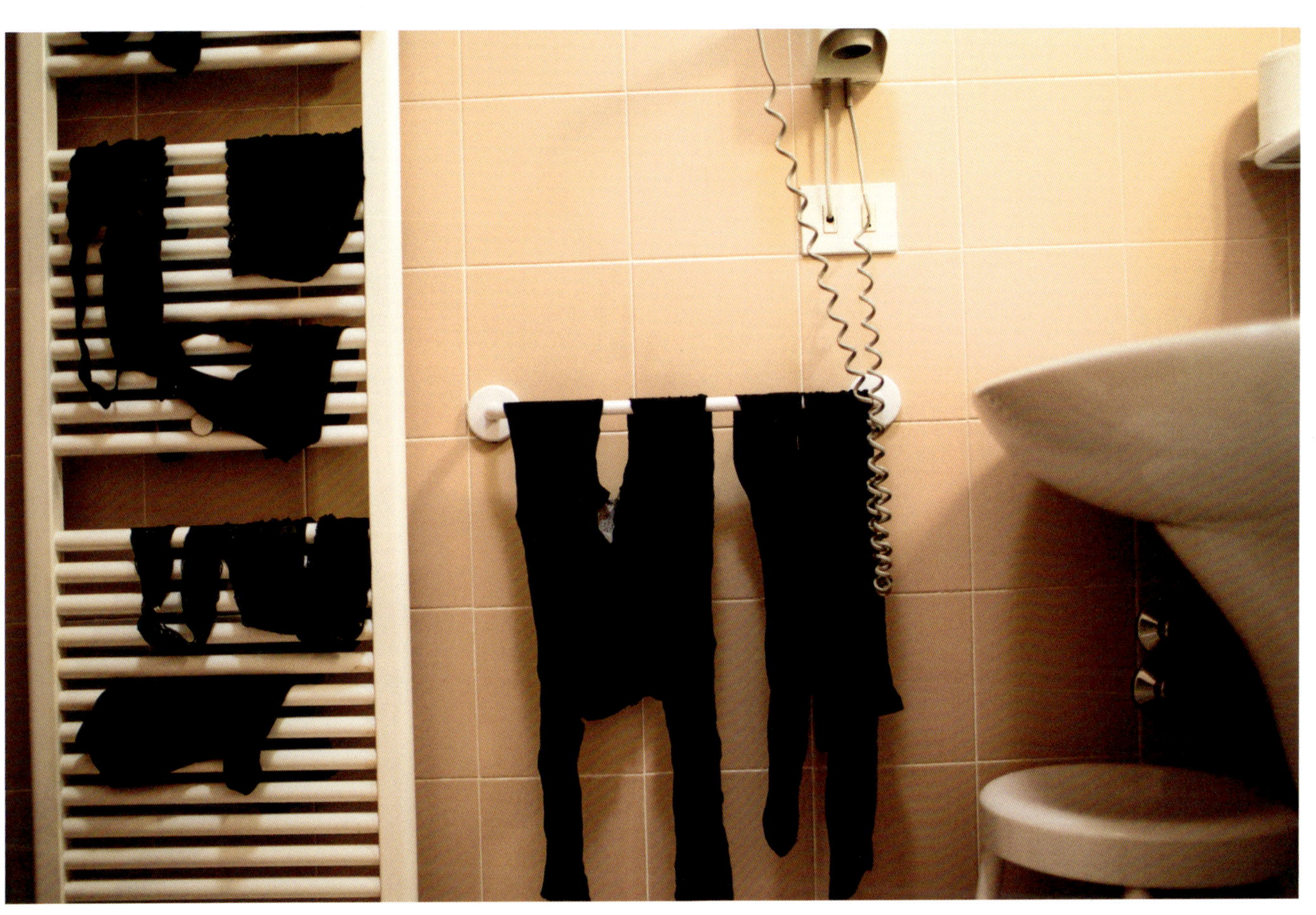

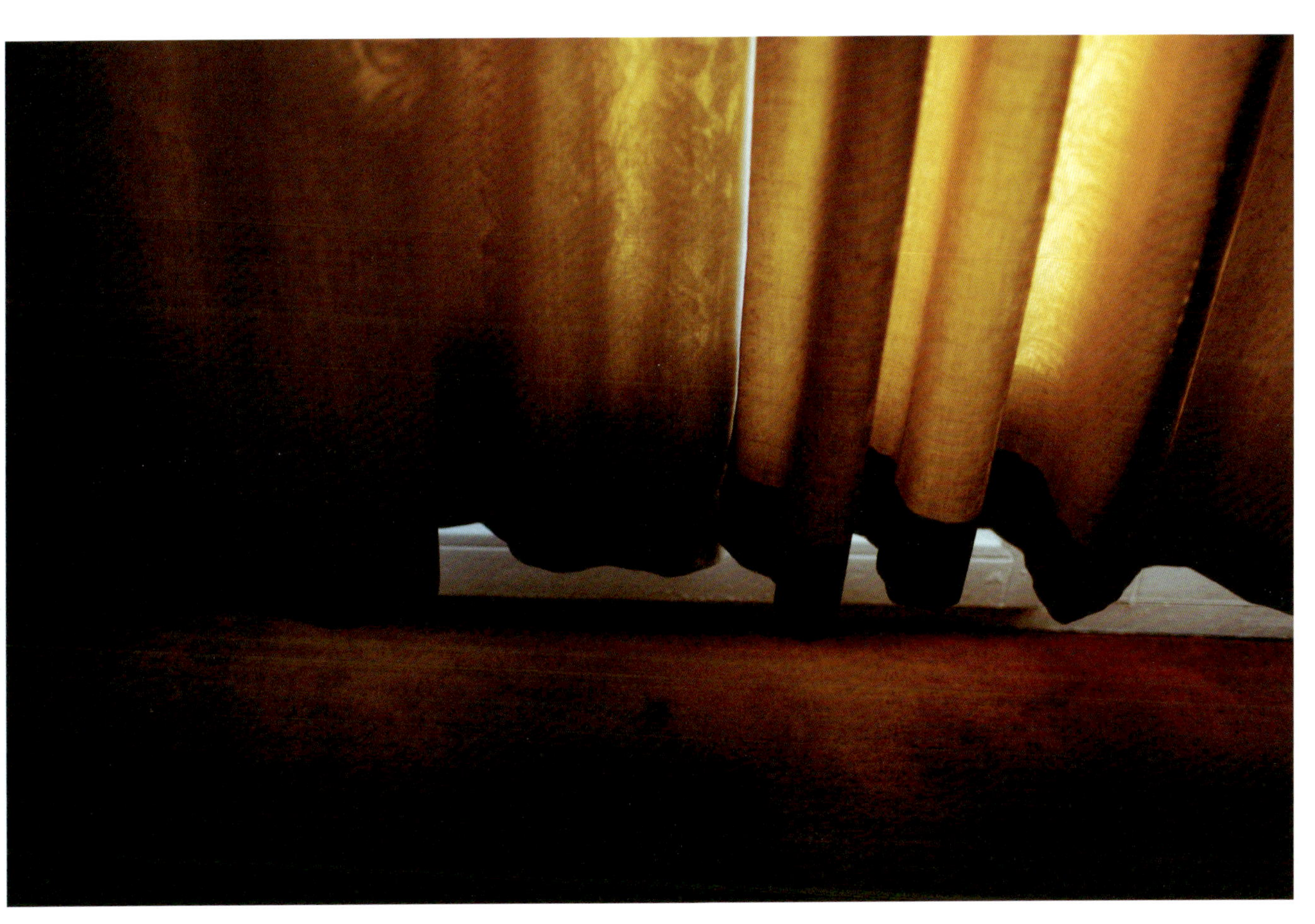

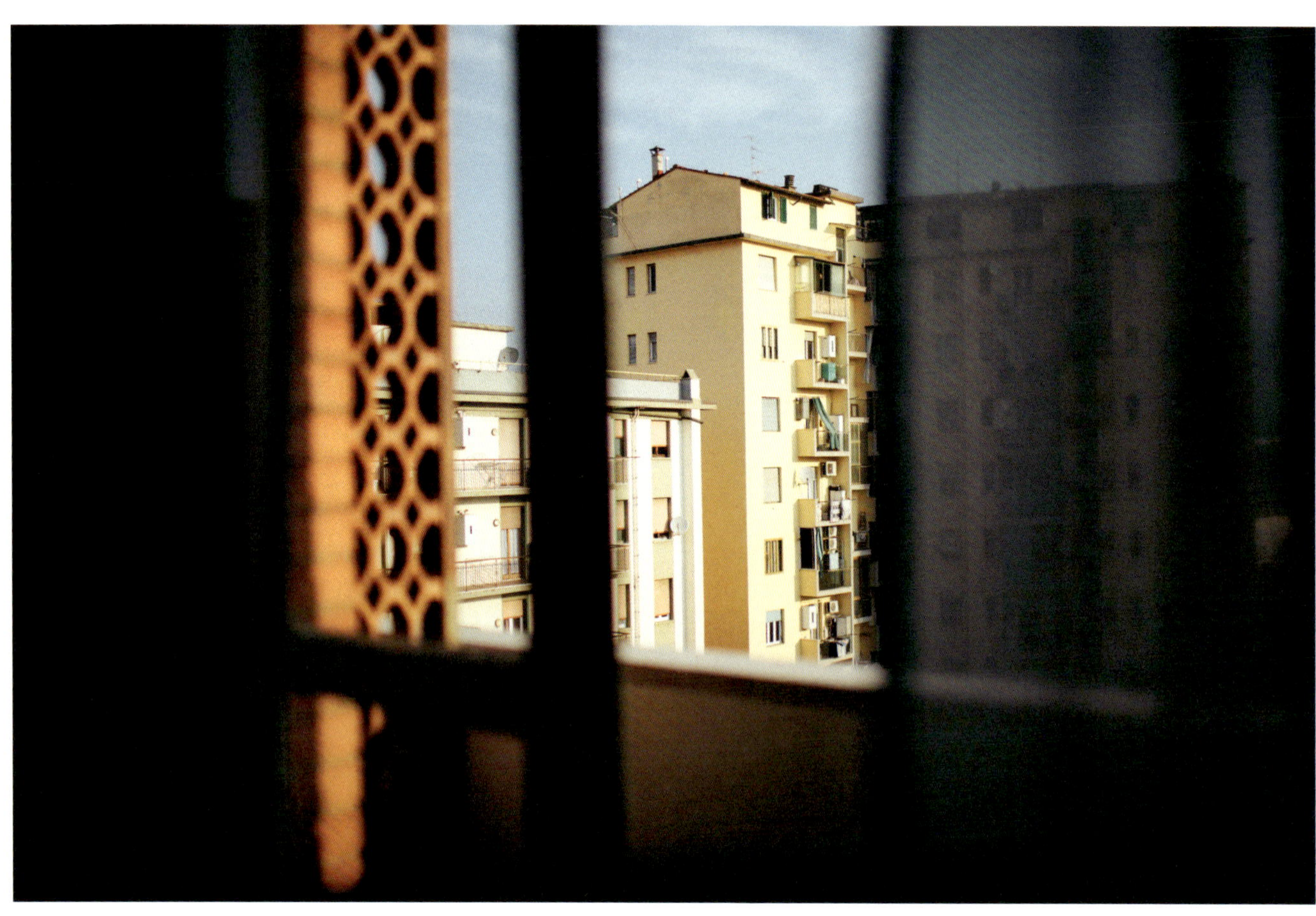

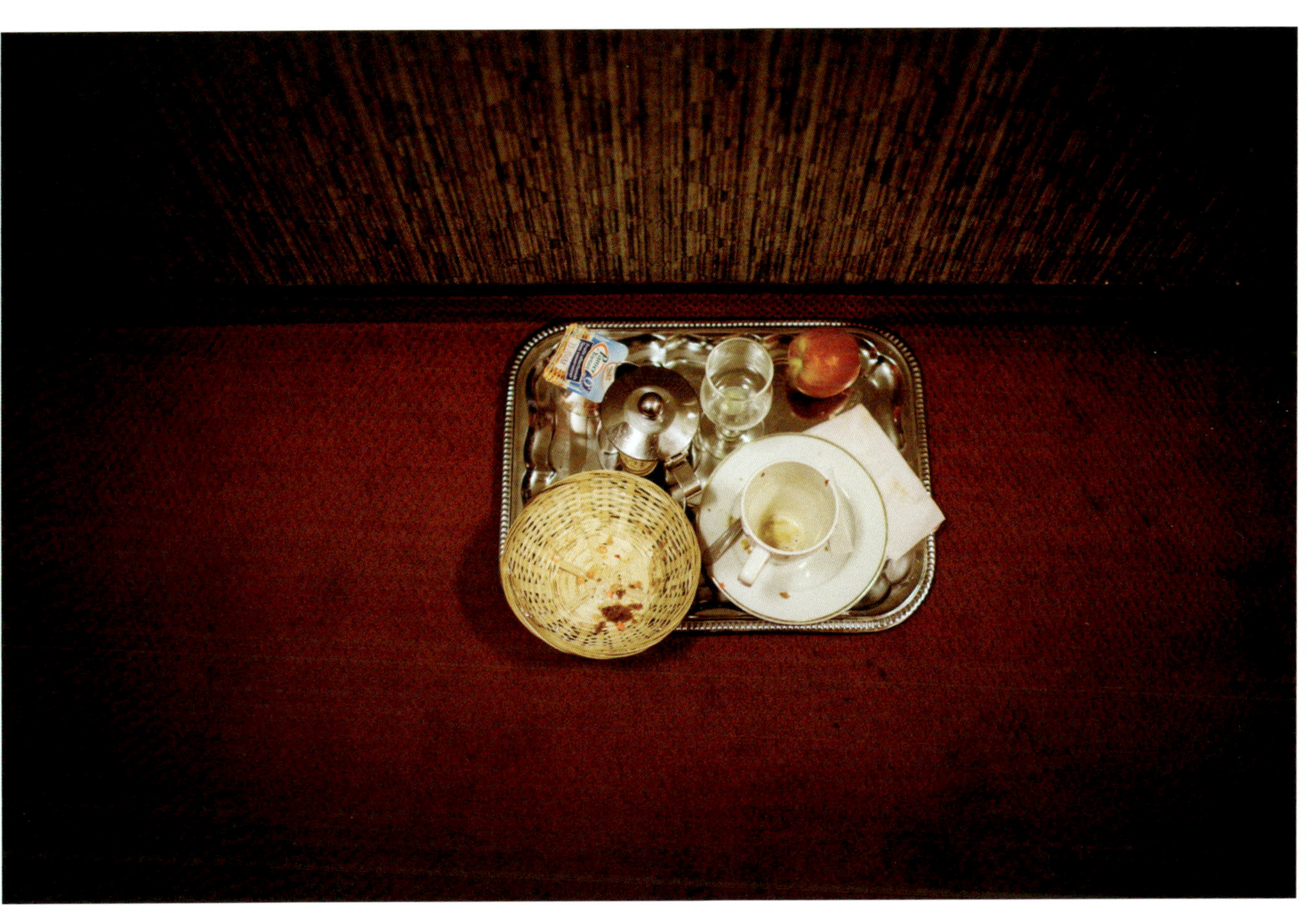

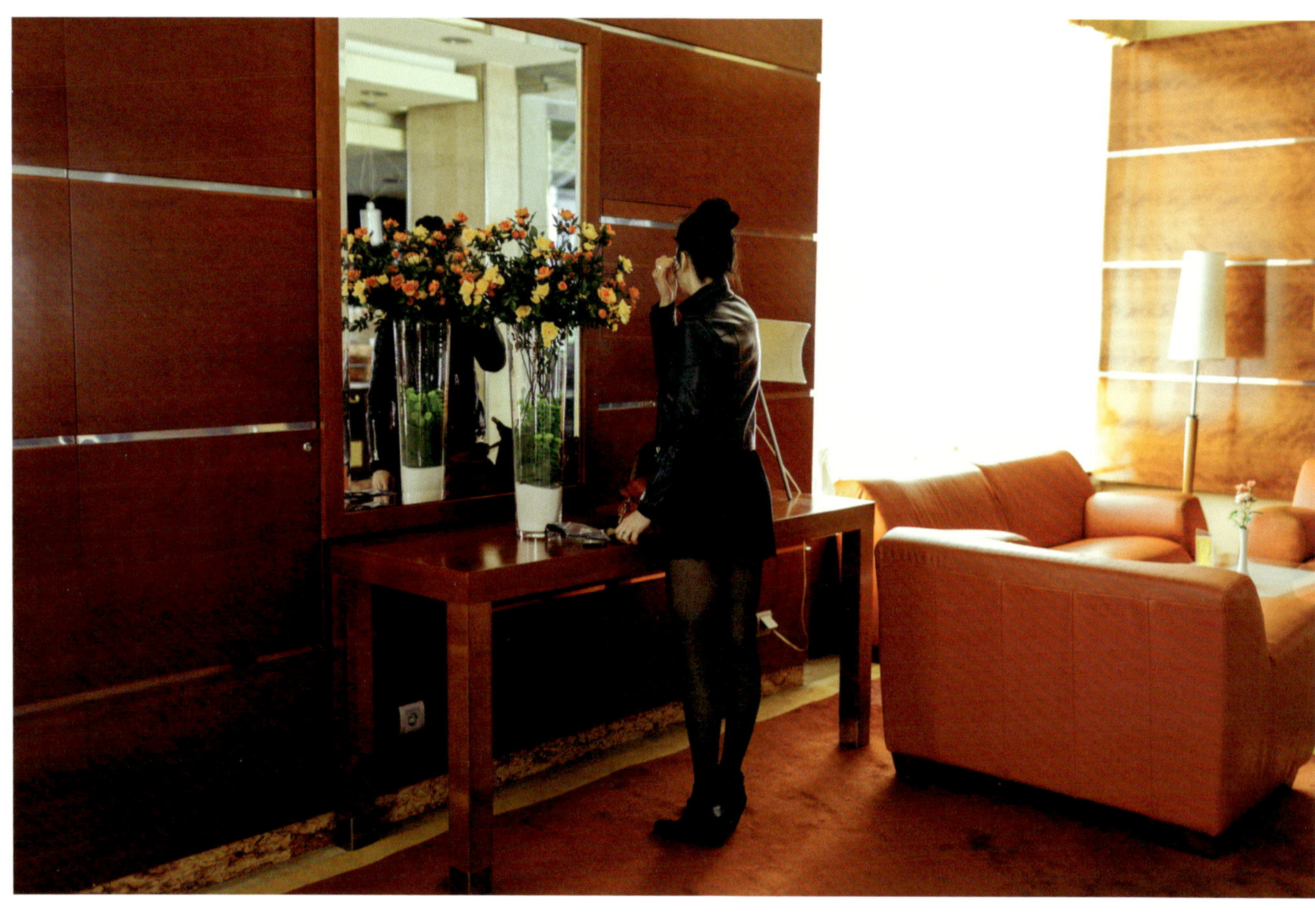

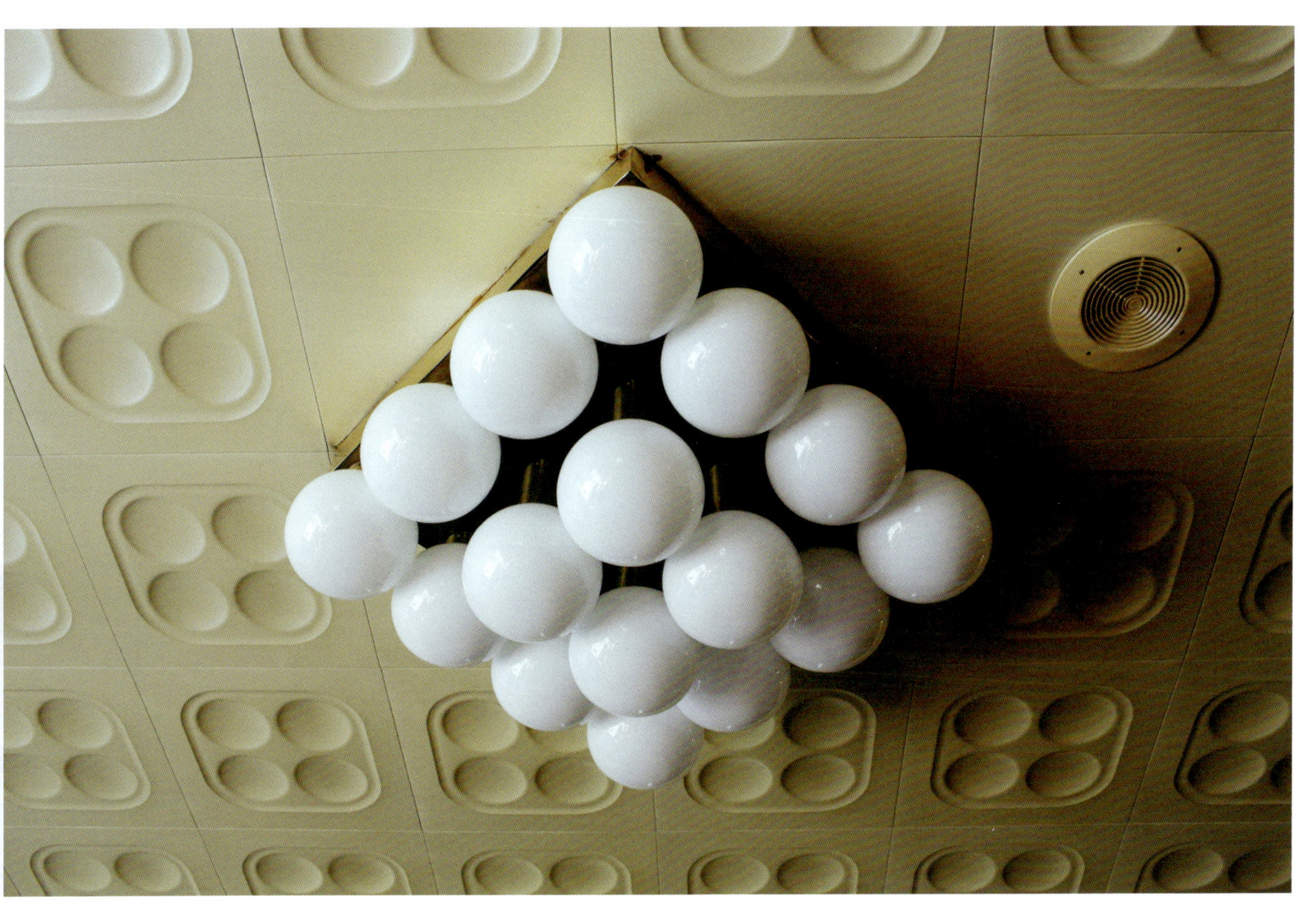

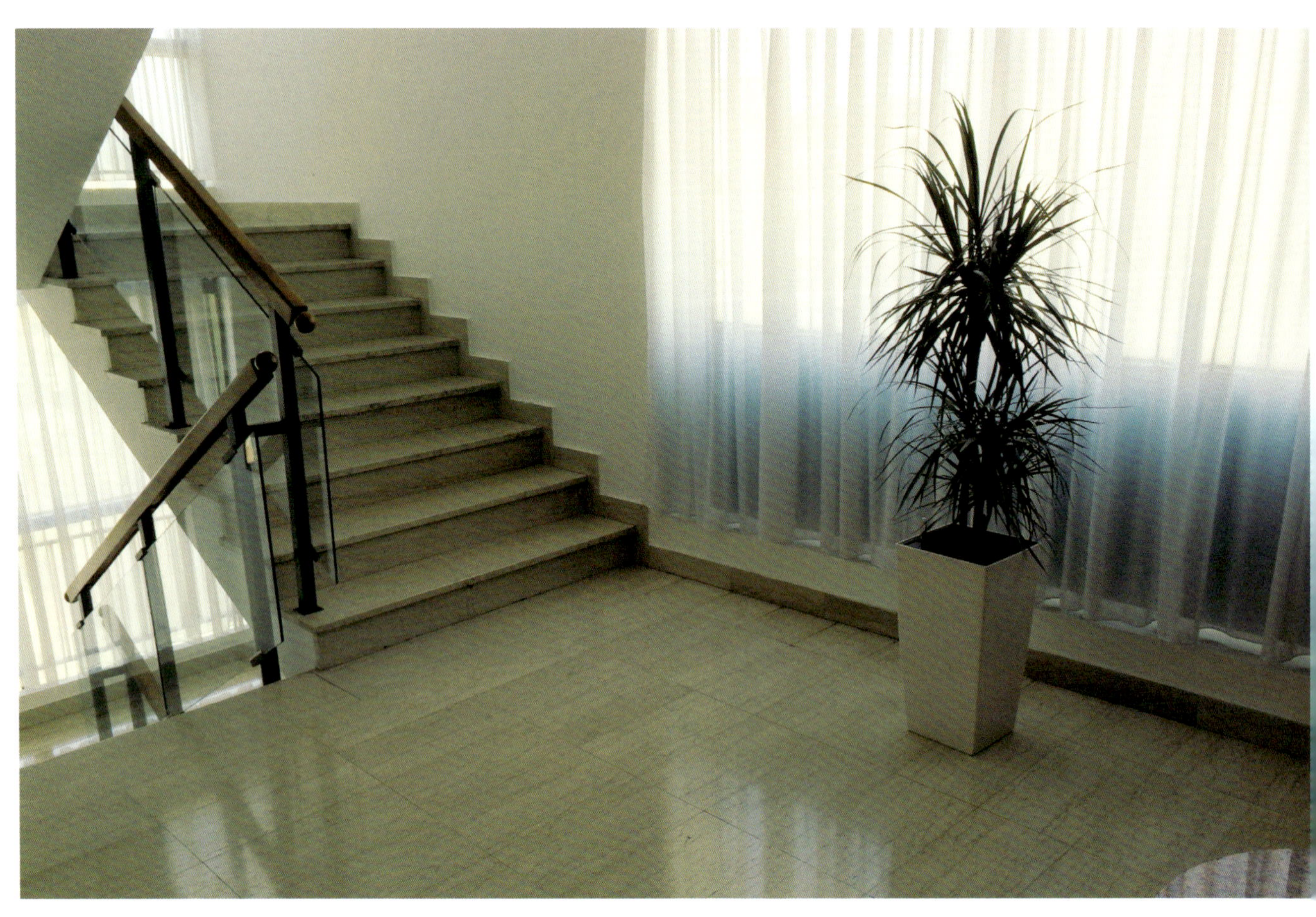

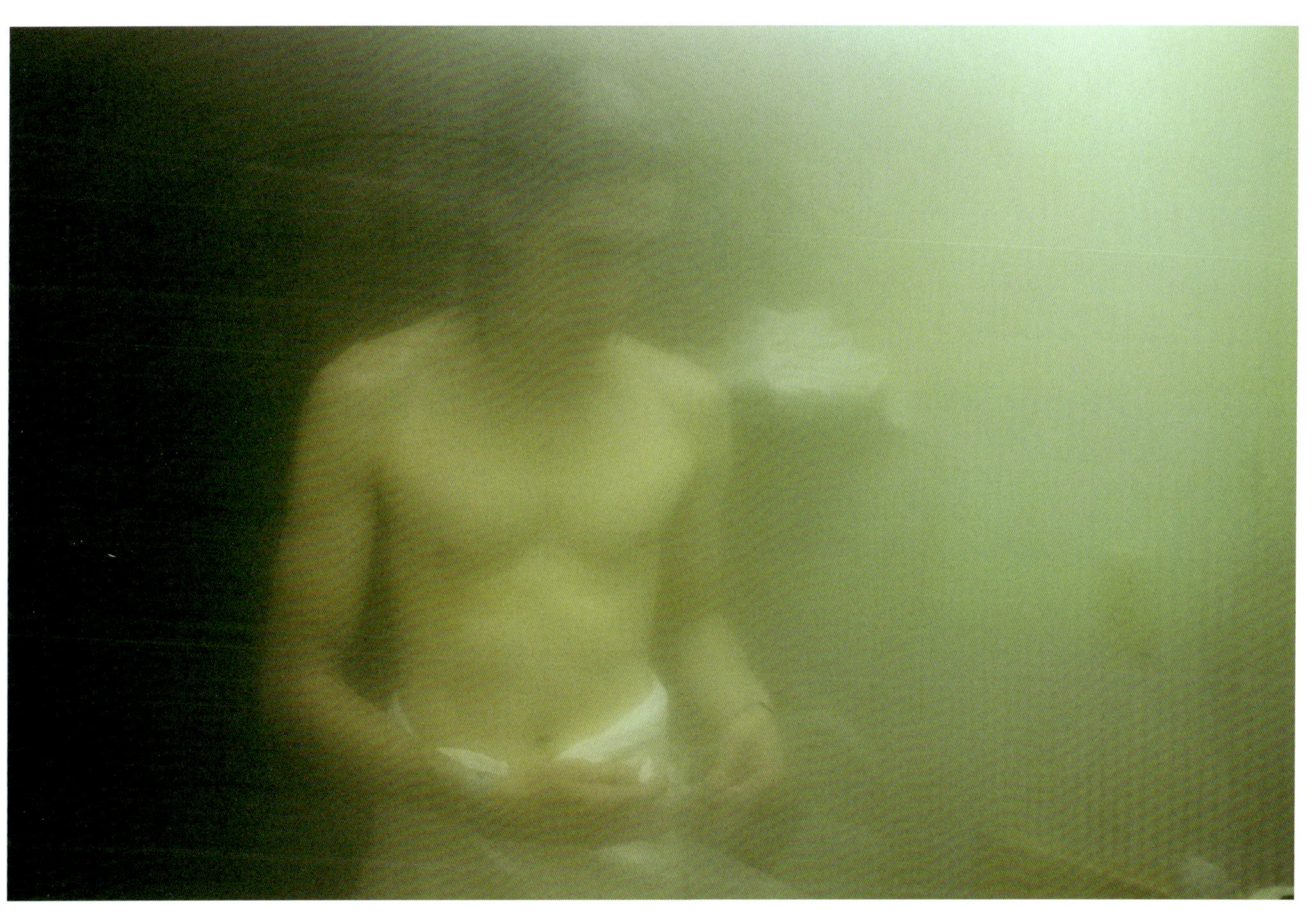

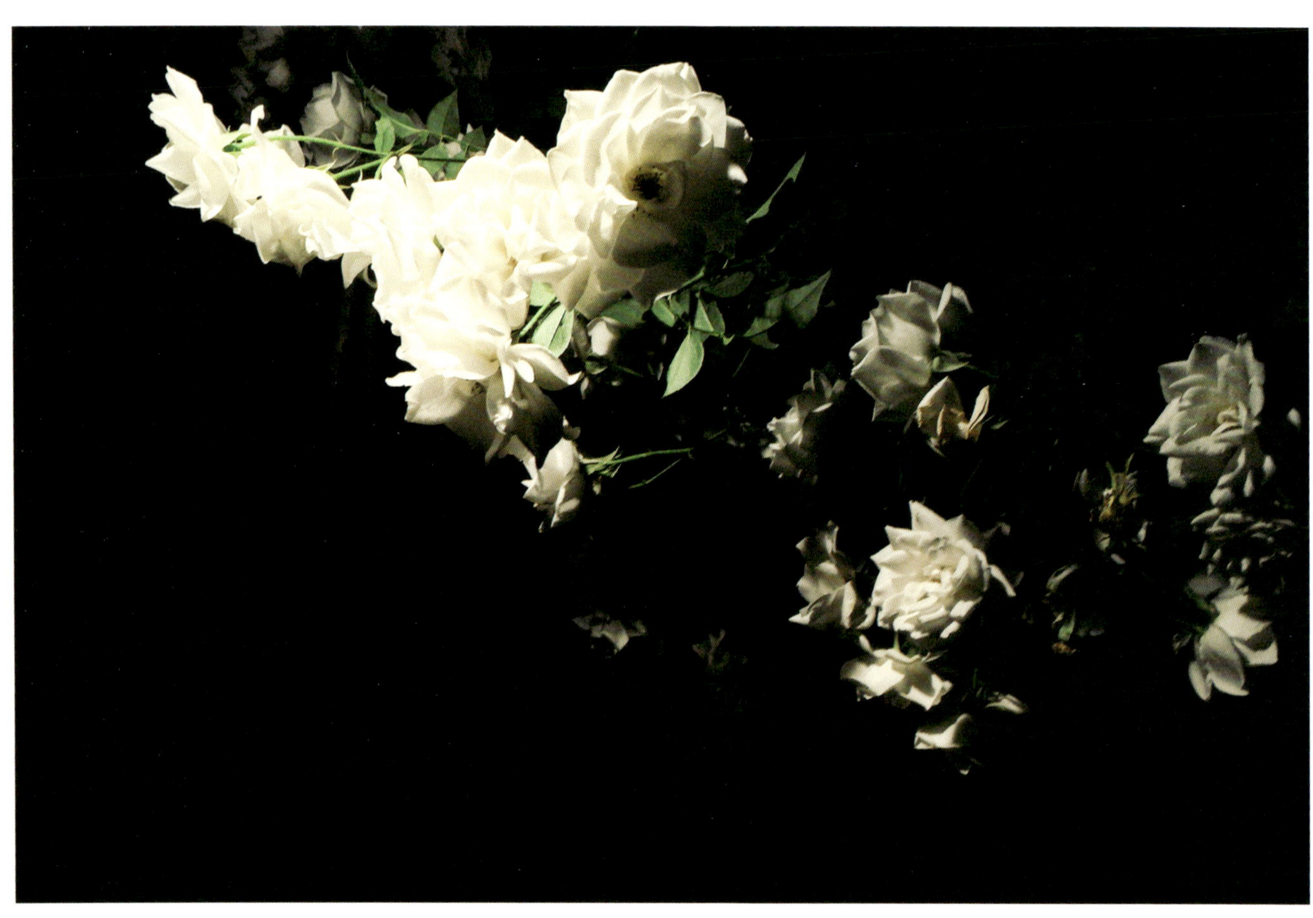

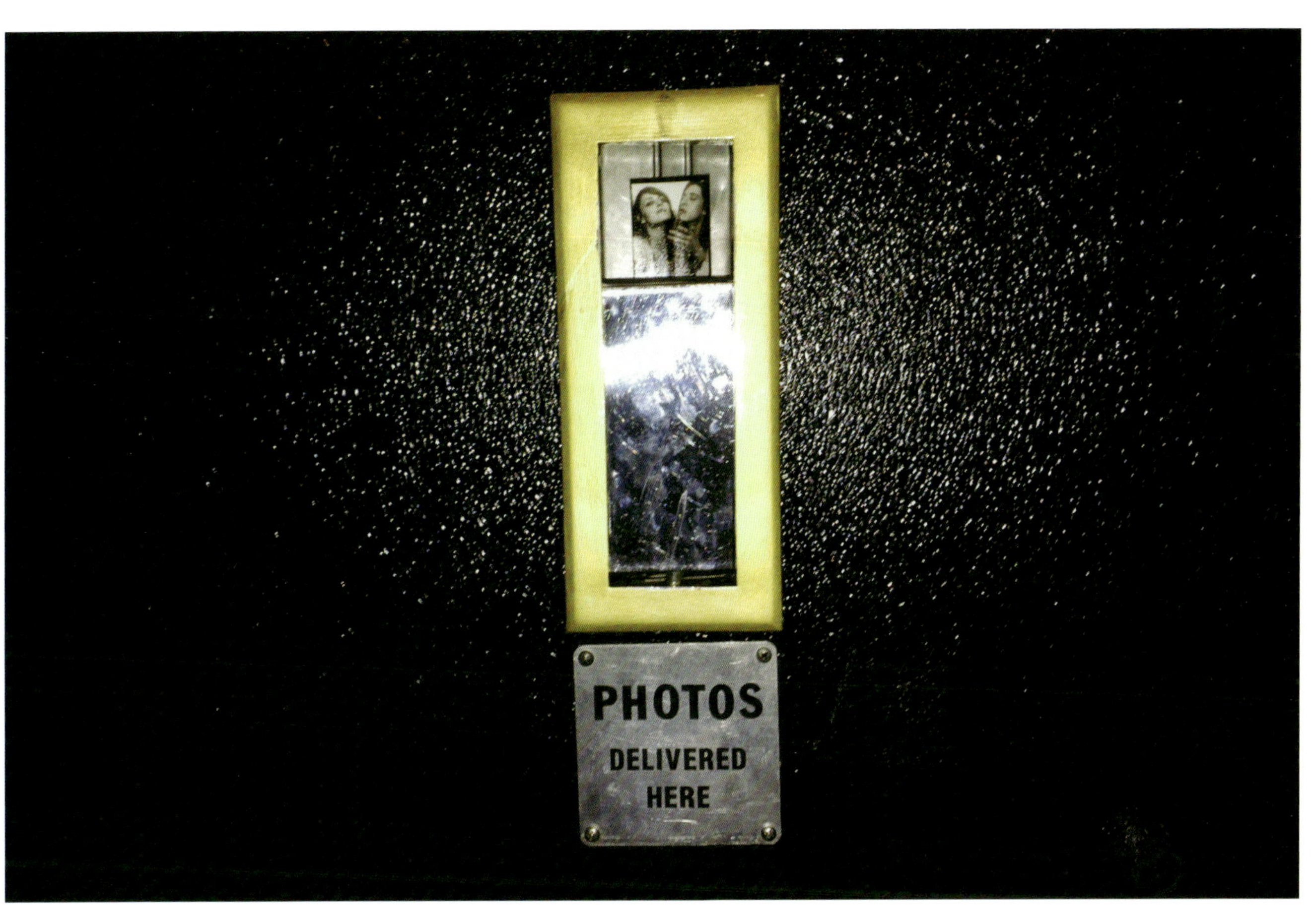
PHOTOS
DELIVERED
HERE

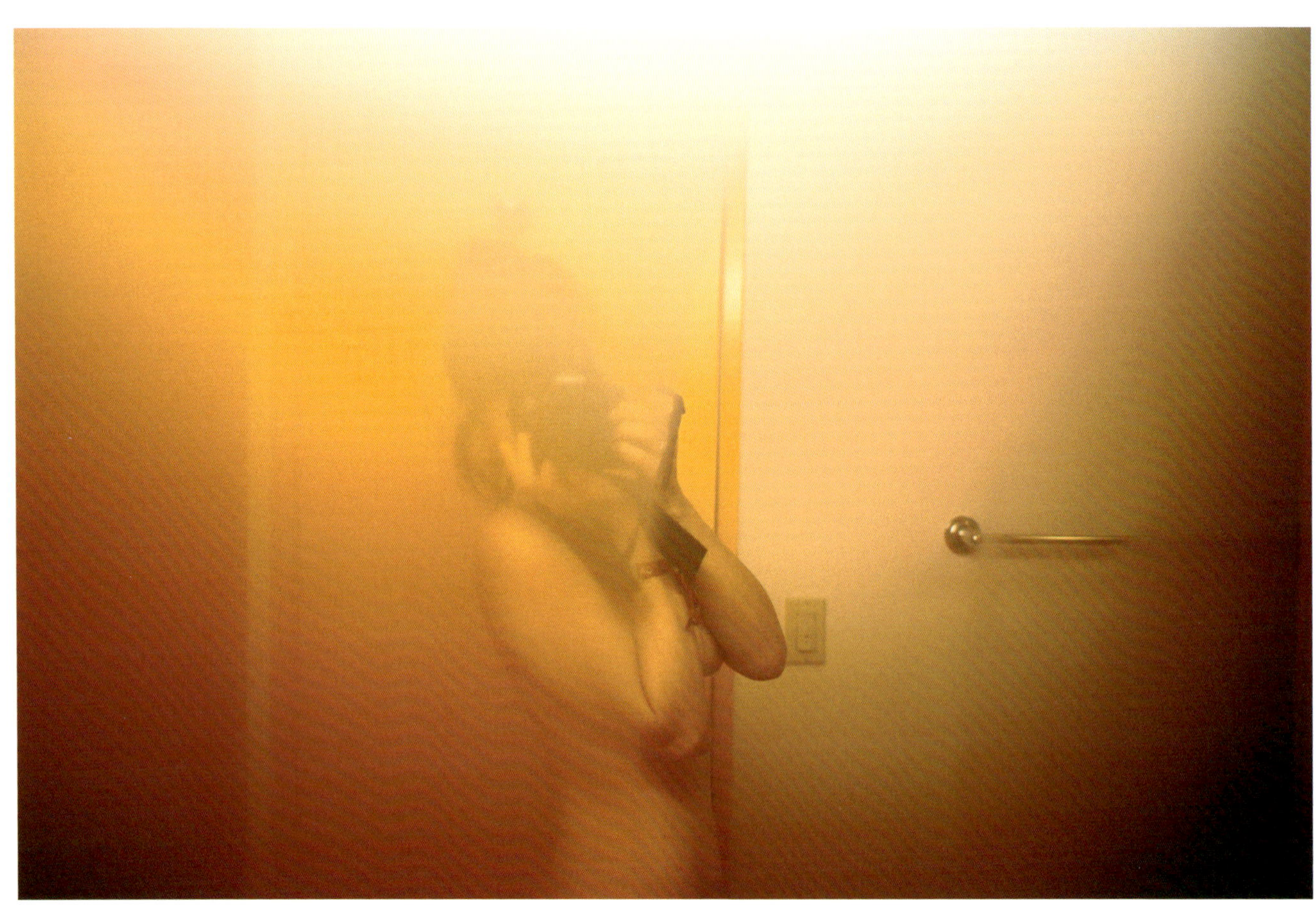

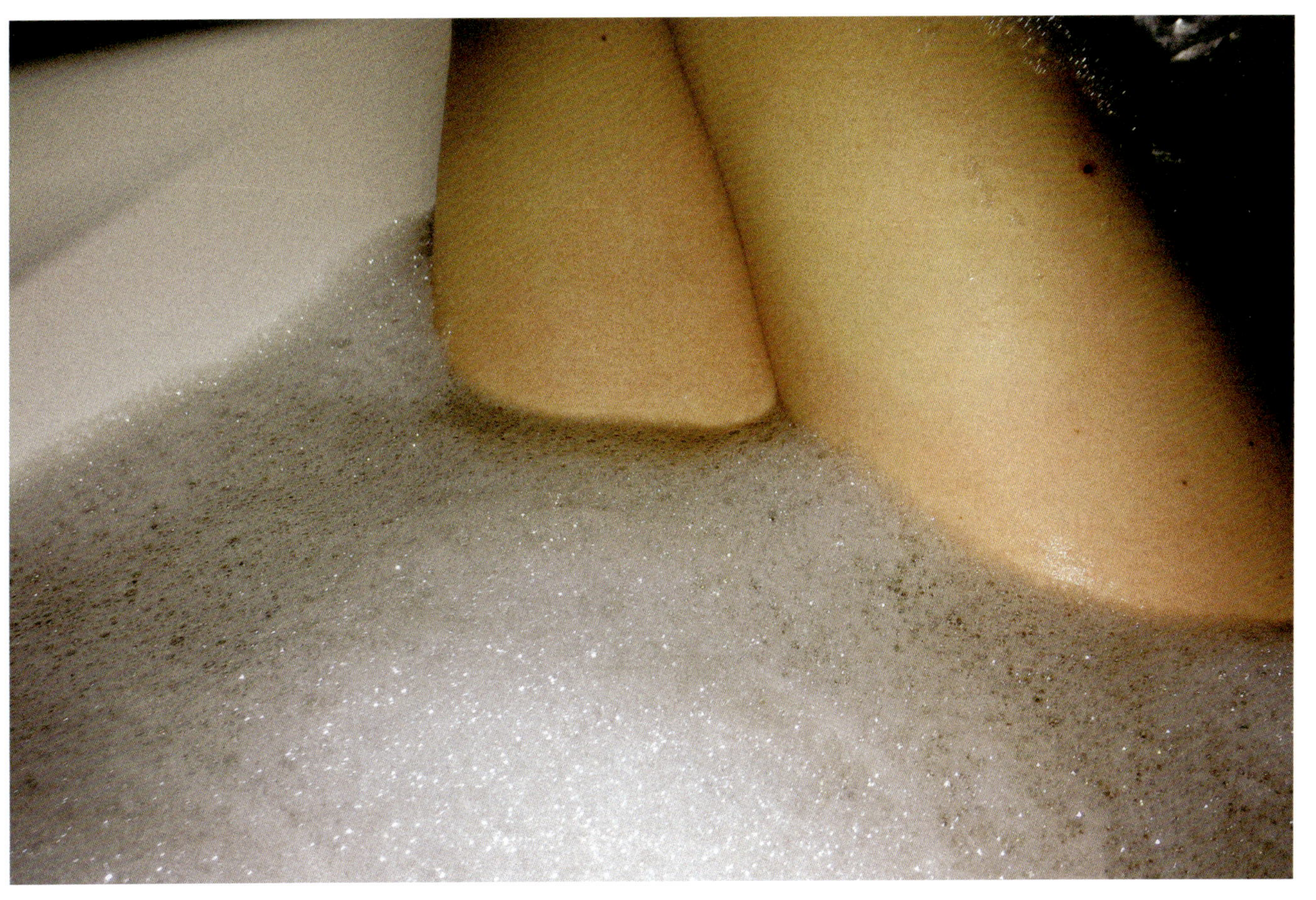

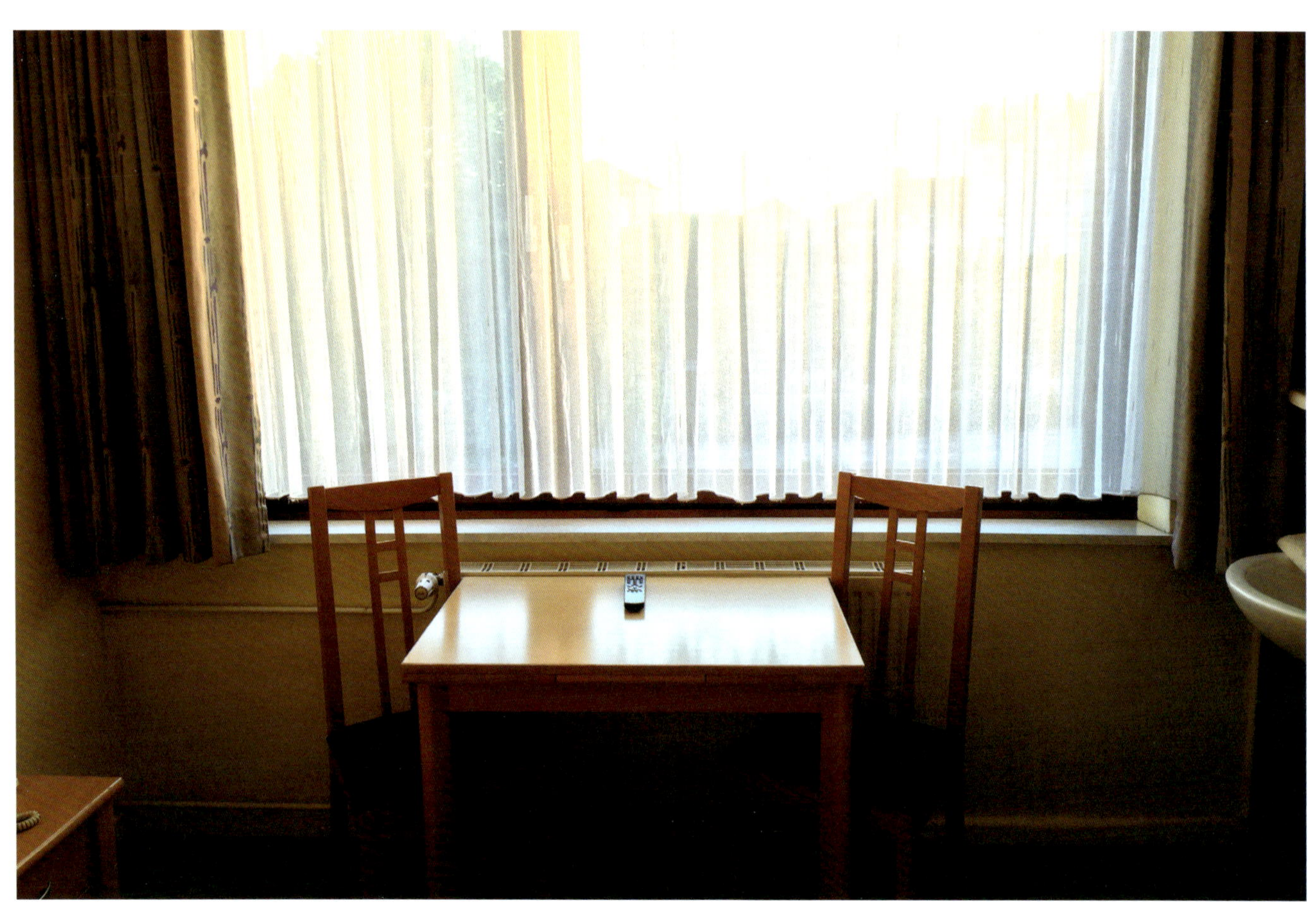

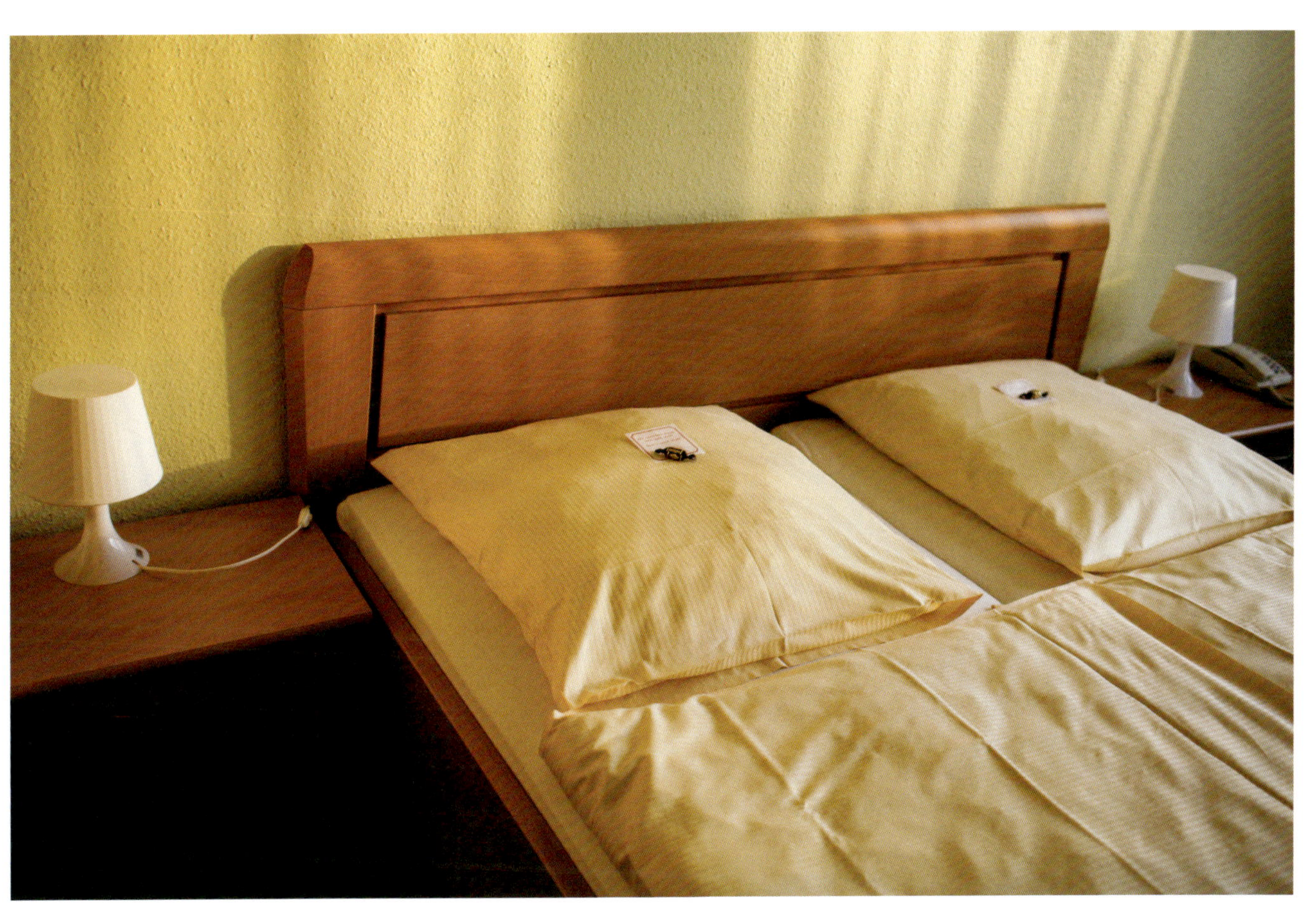

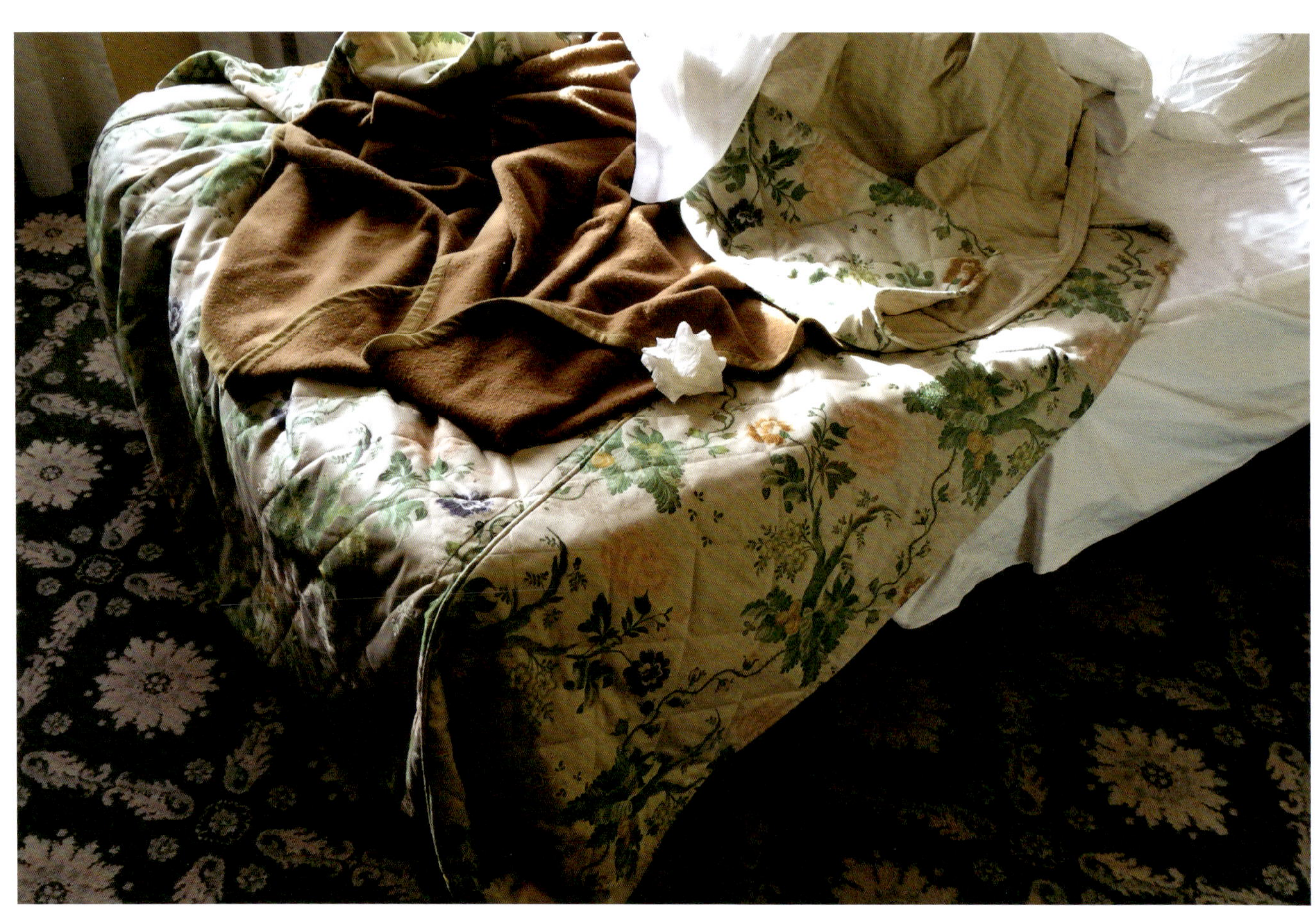

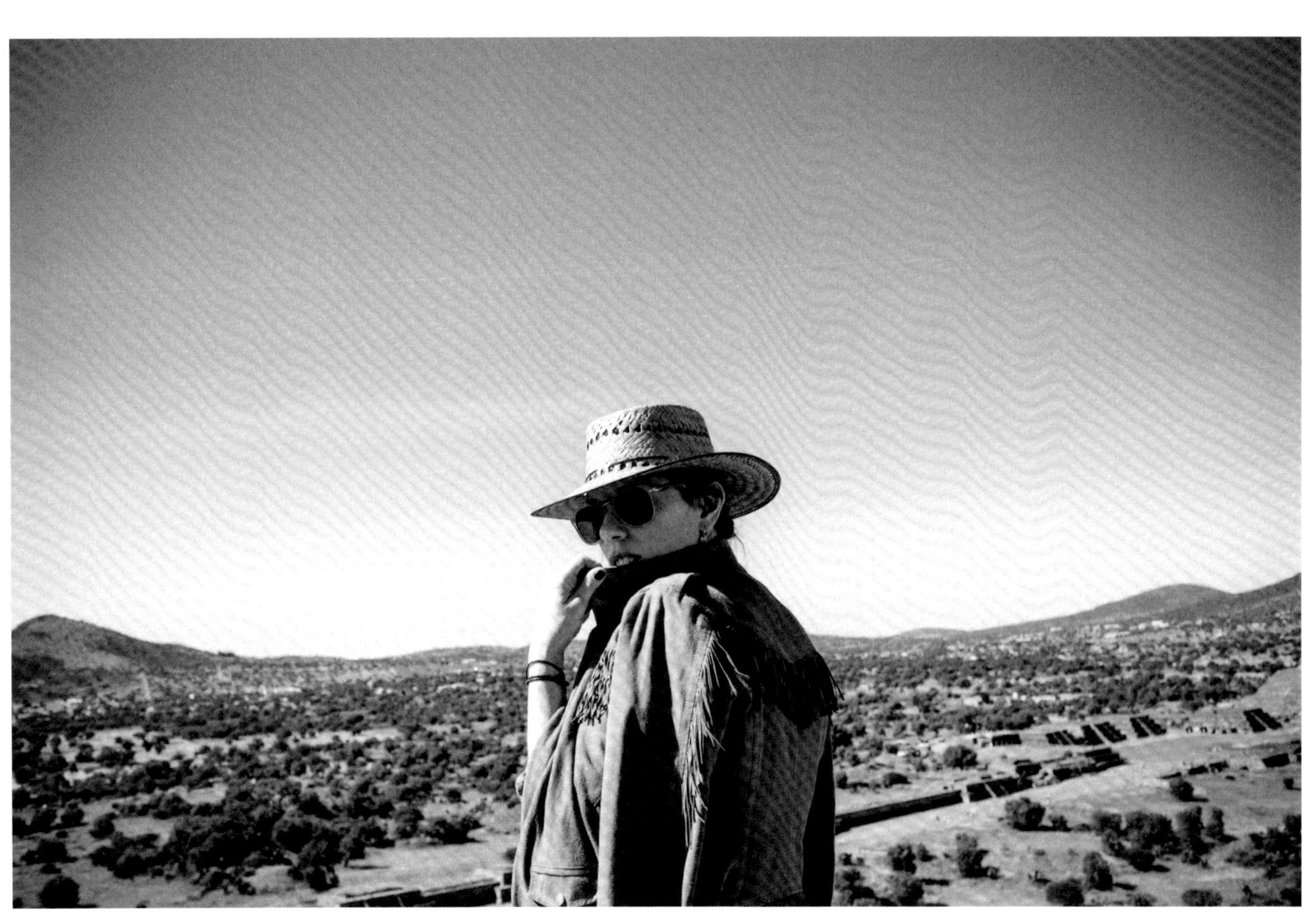

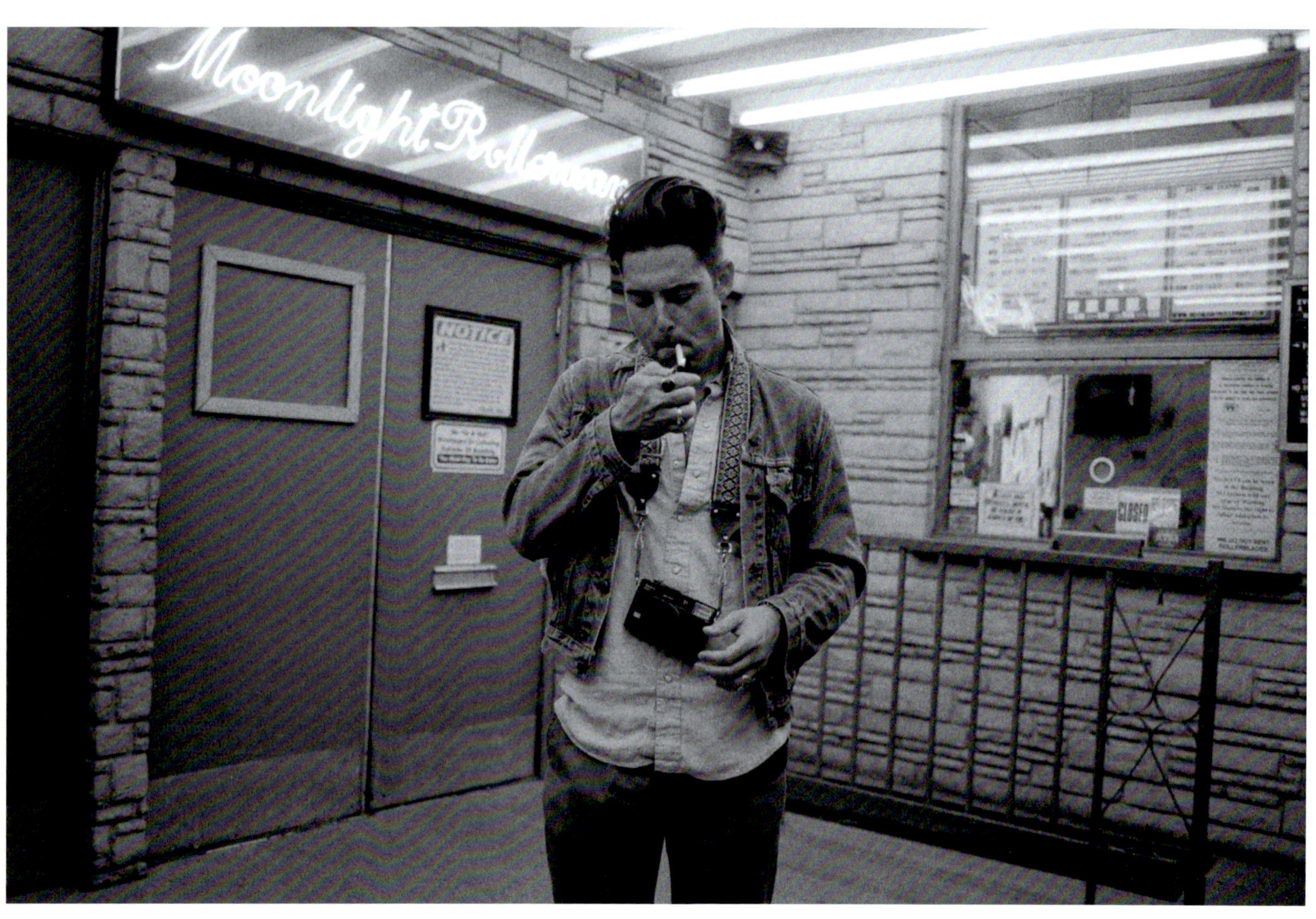
Moonlight
NOTICE
CLOSED

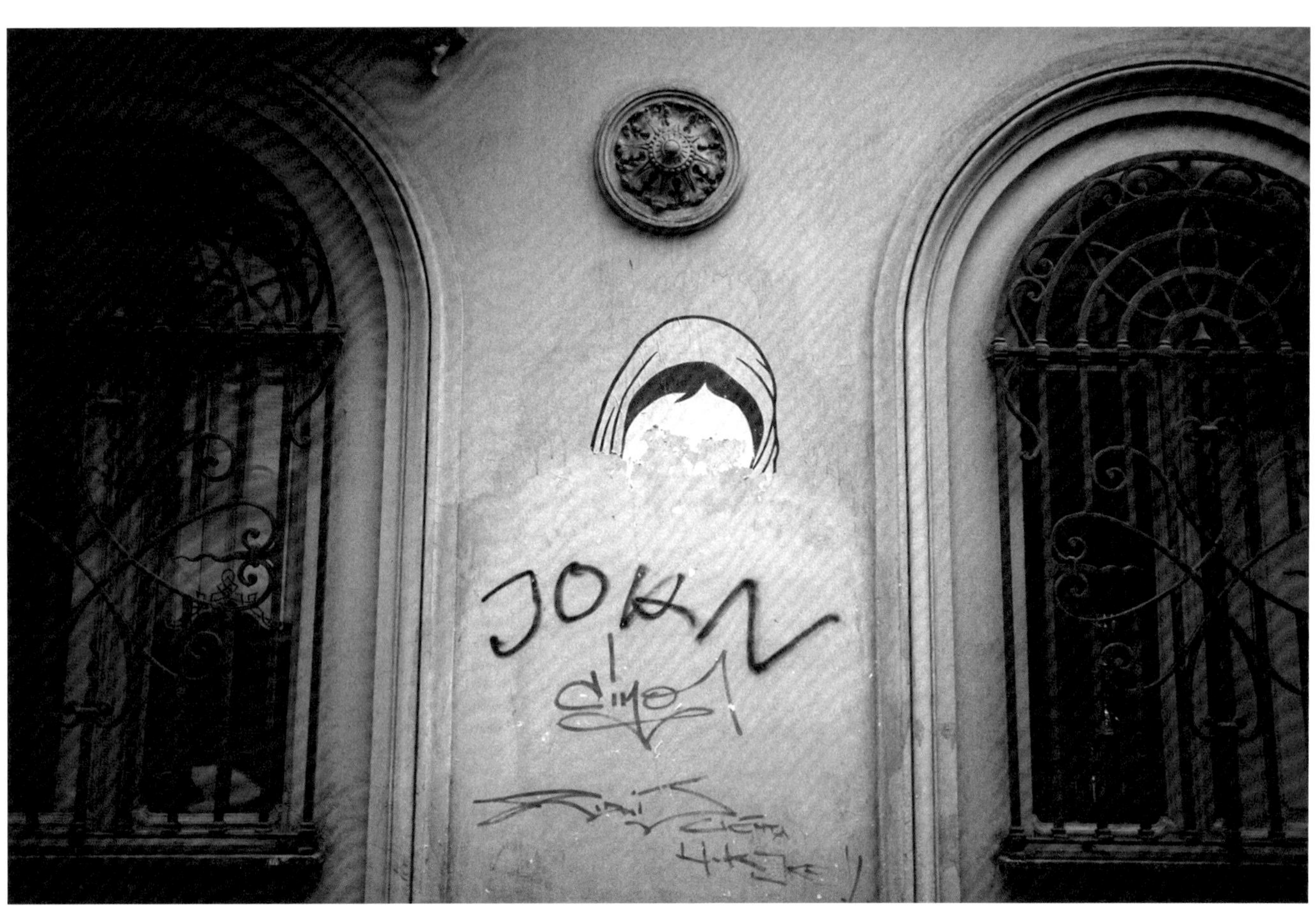

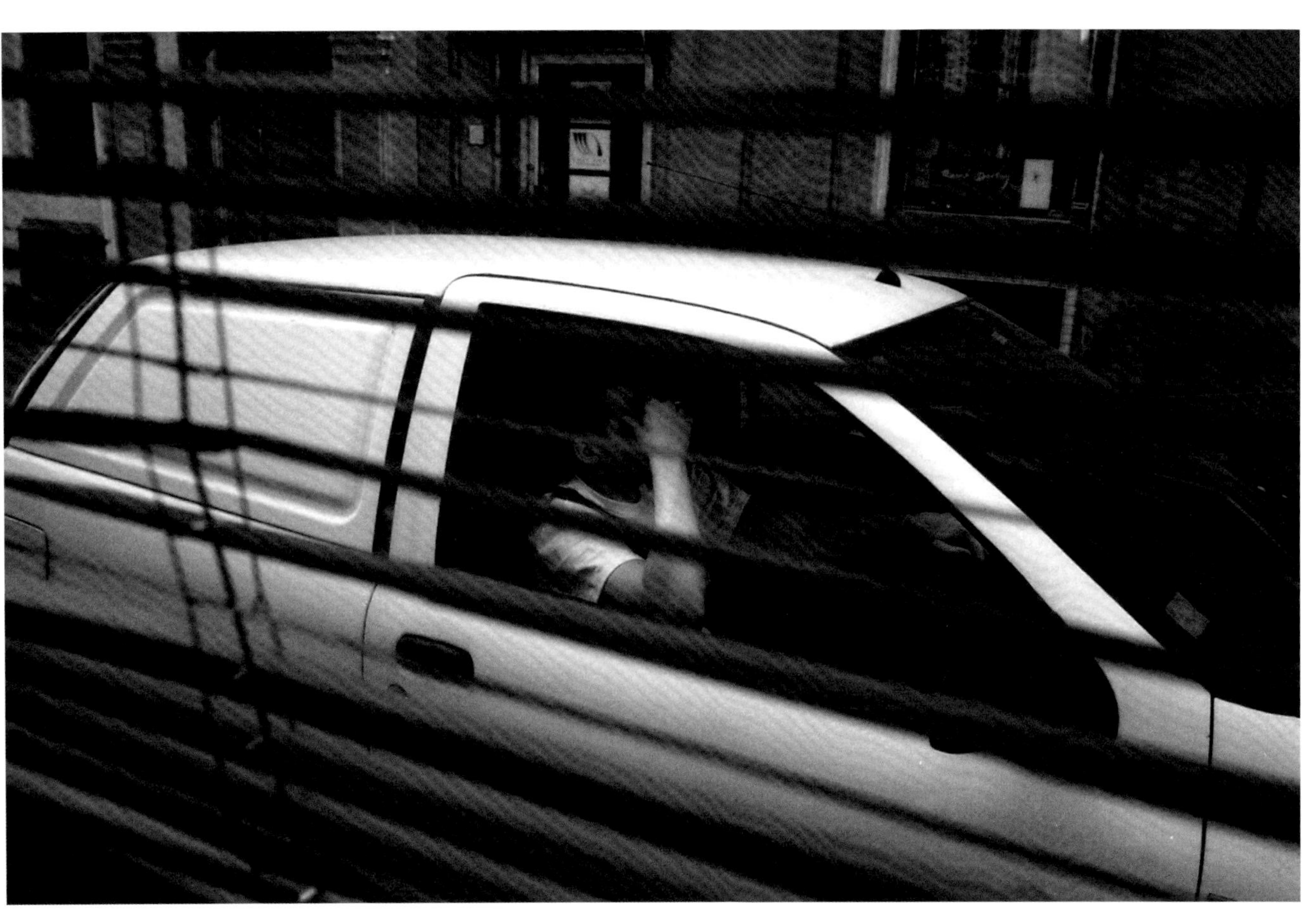

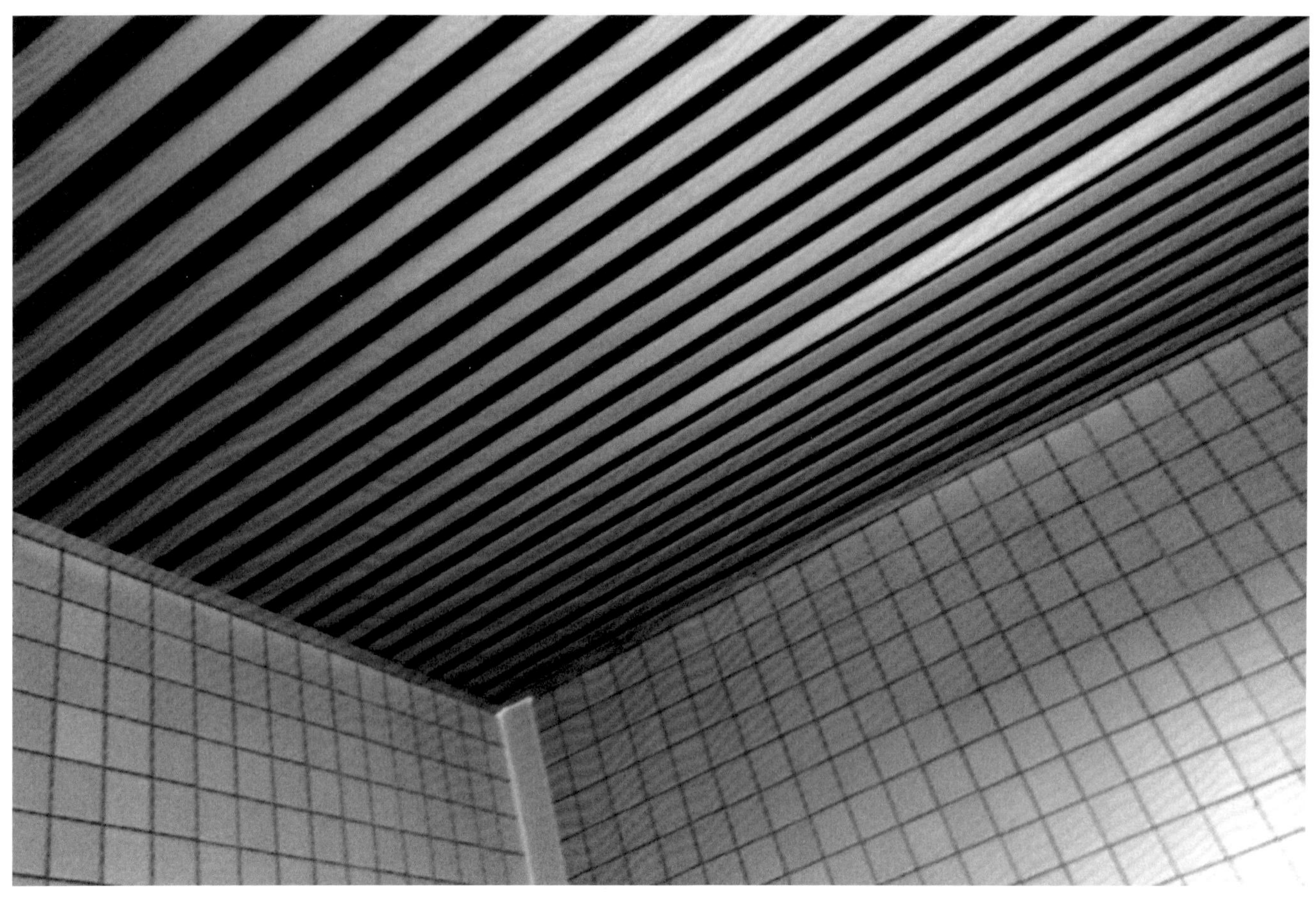

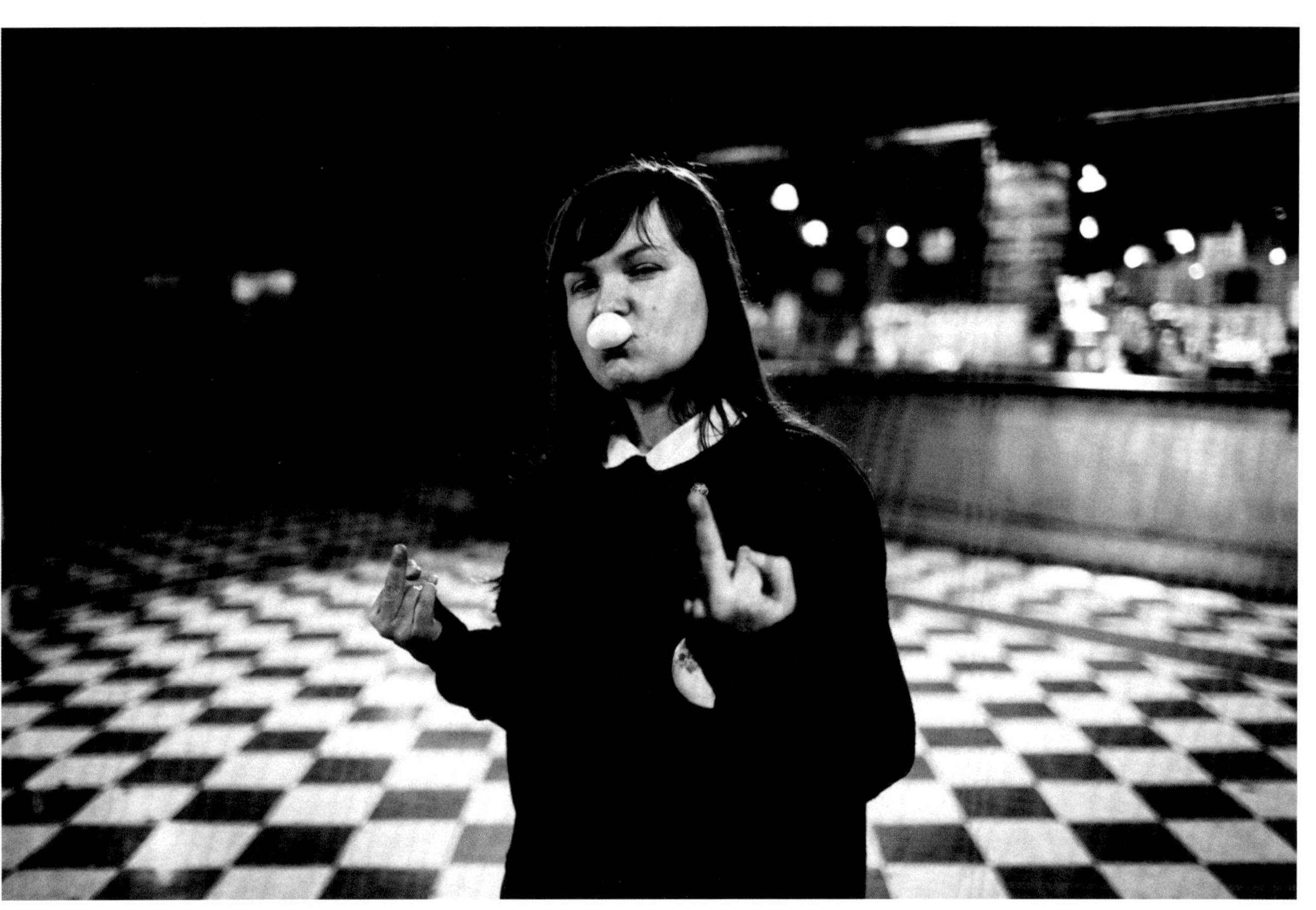

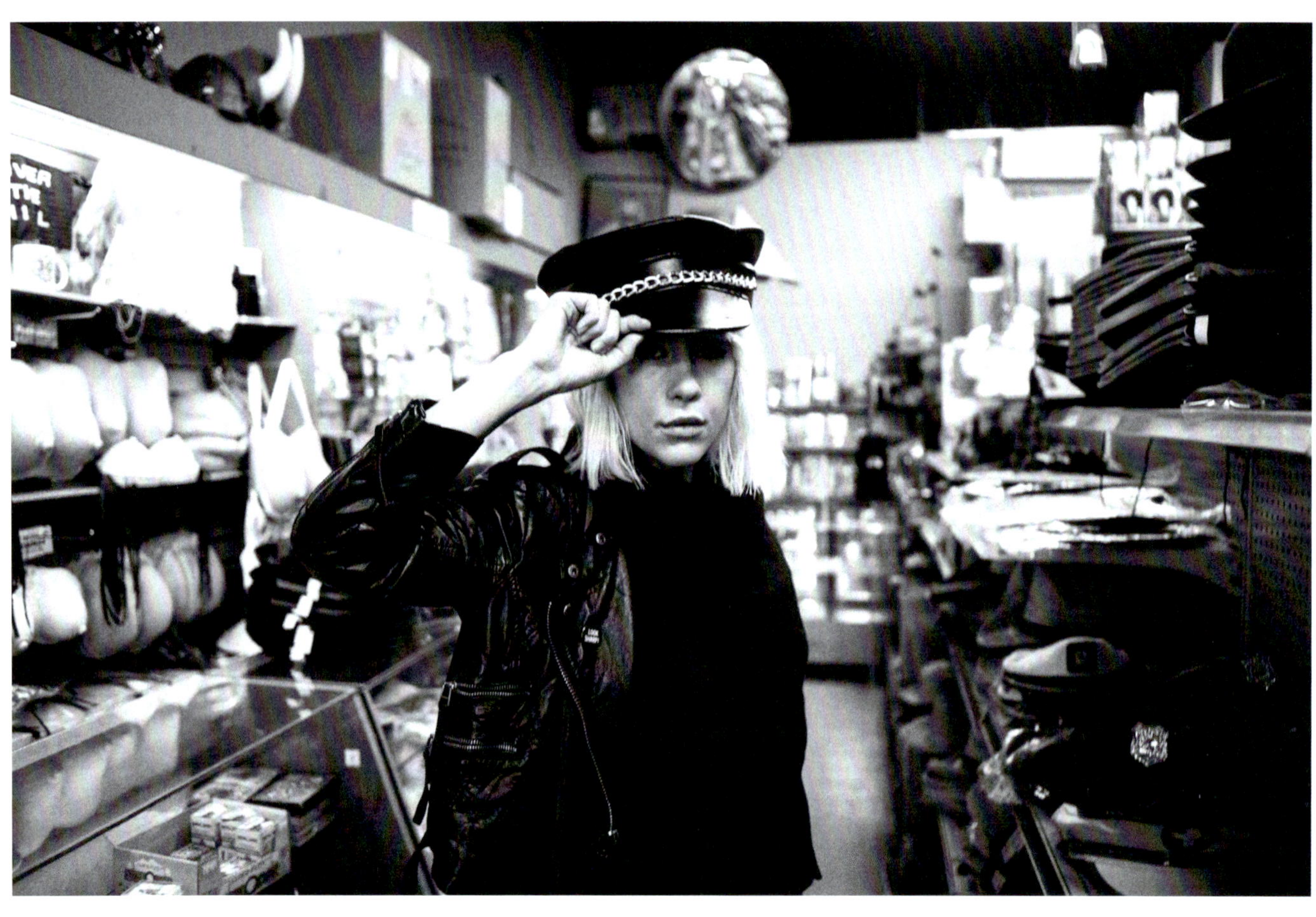

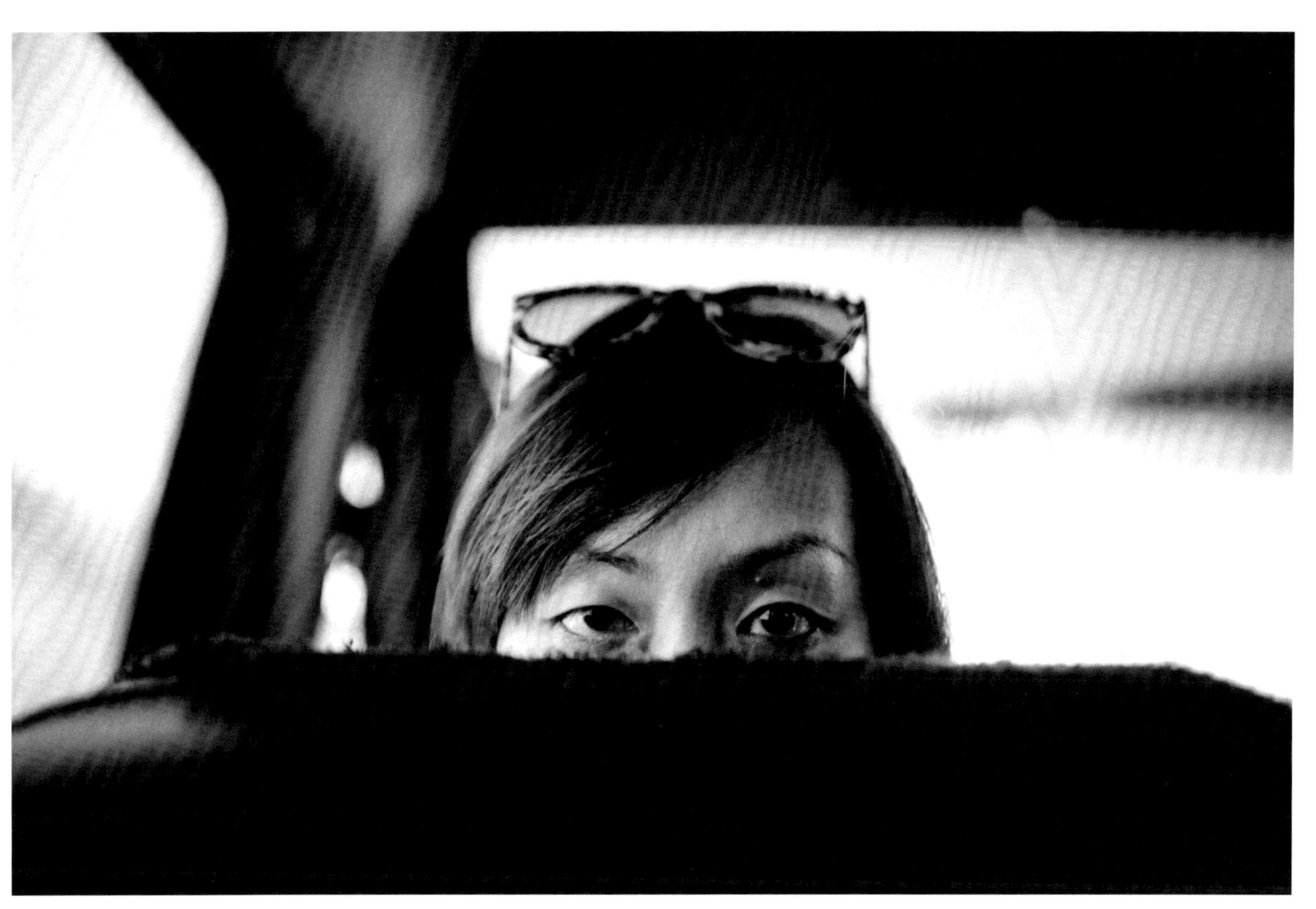

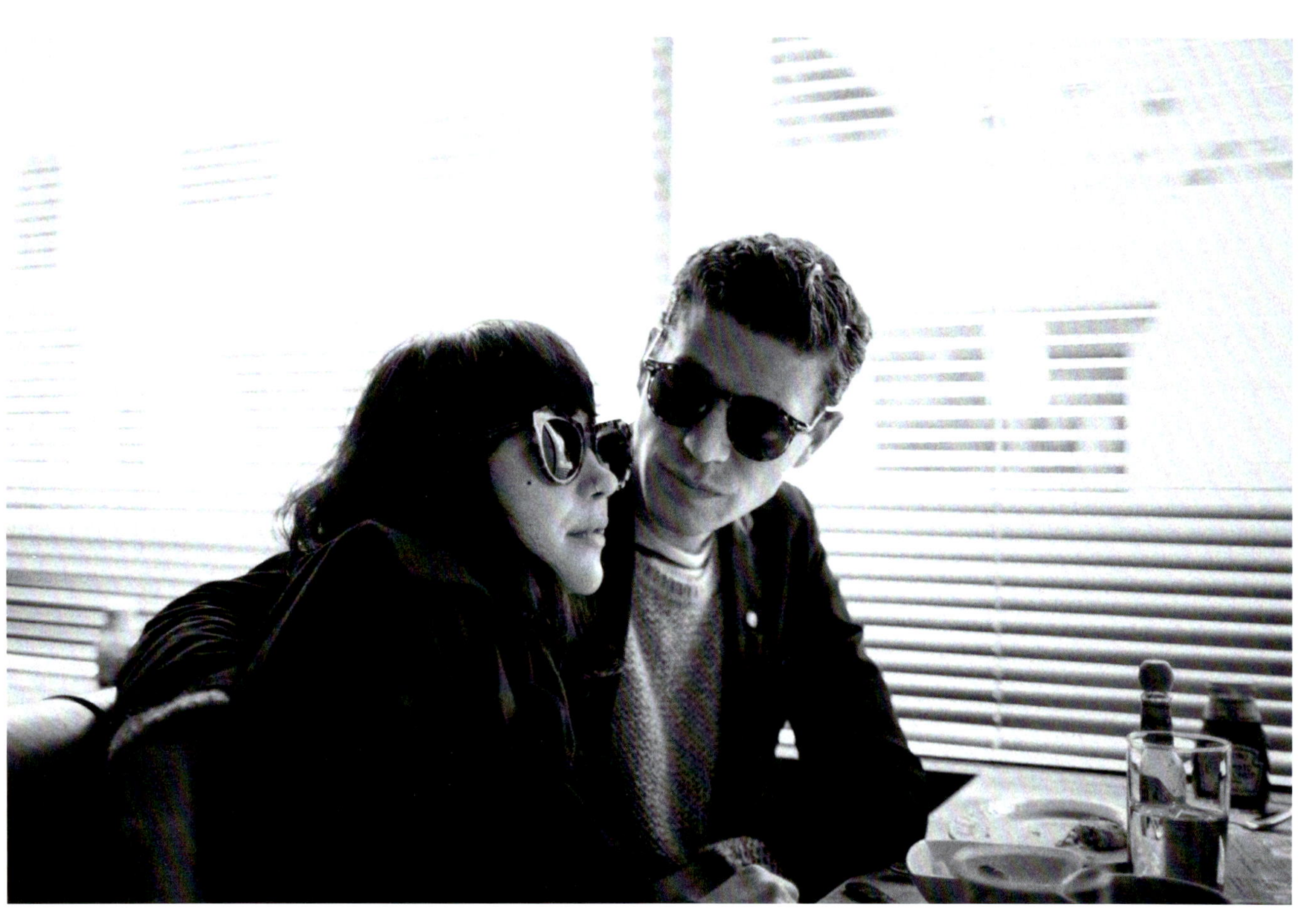

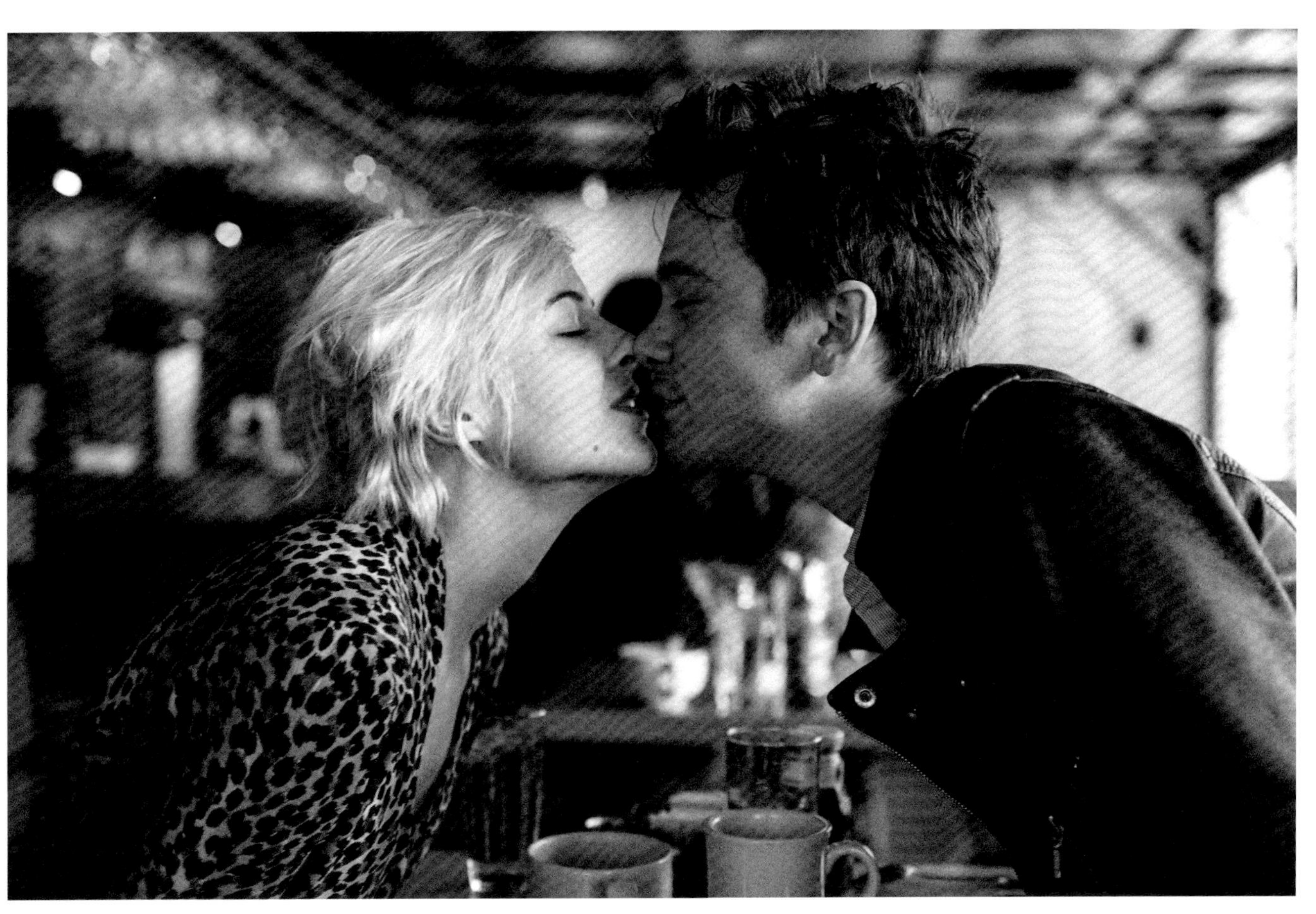

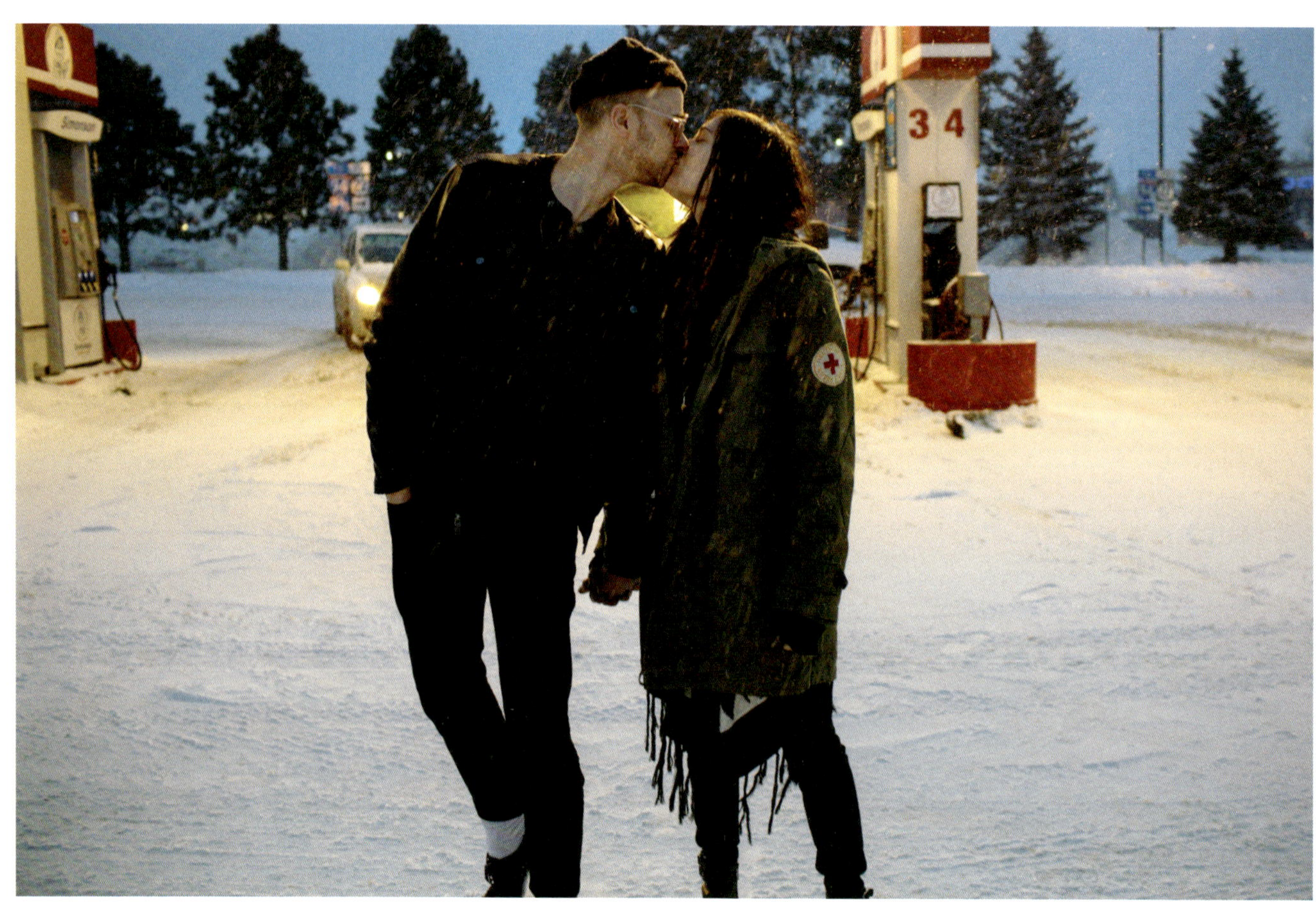
3 4

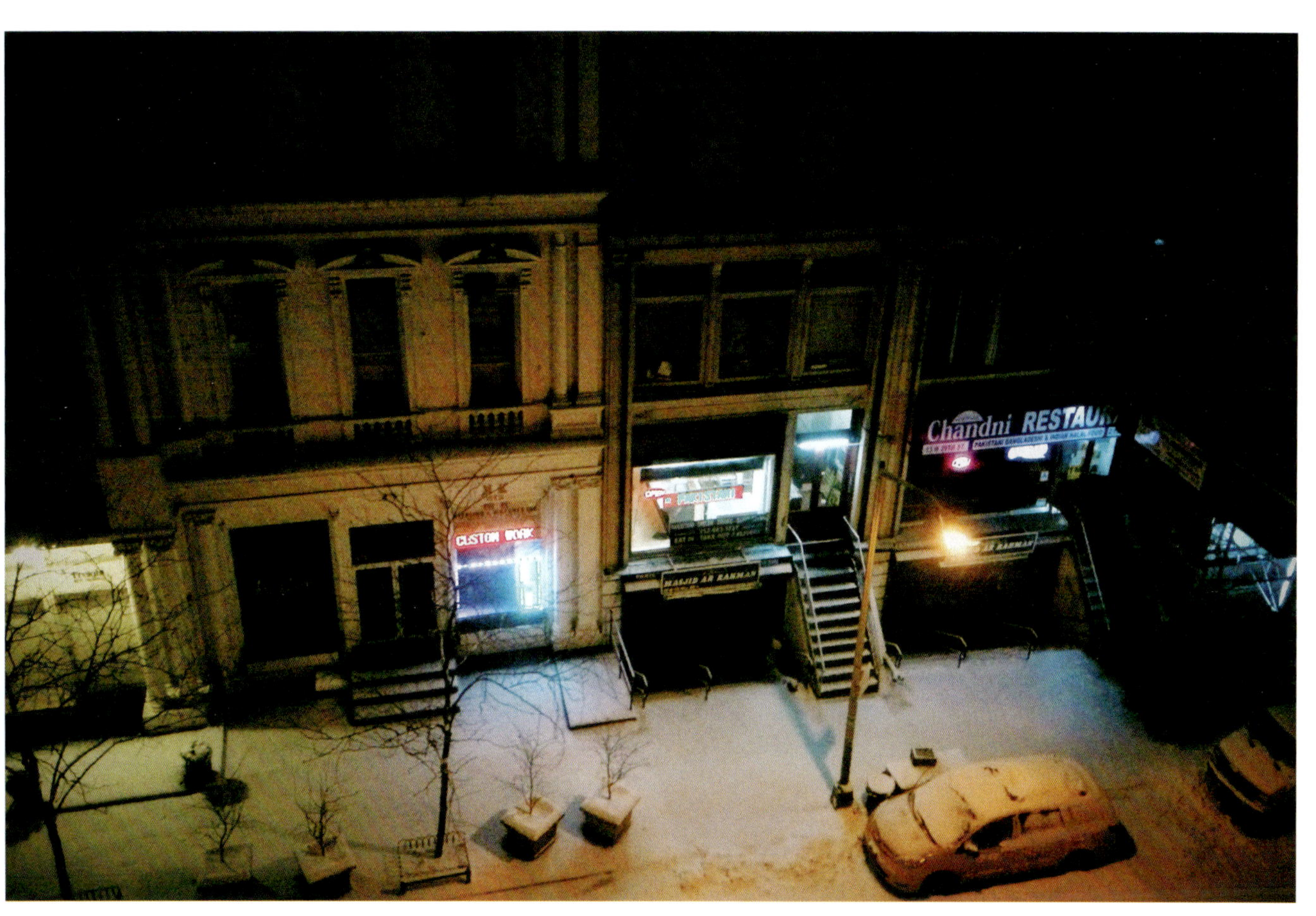
CUSTOM WORK
MASJID AR RAHMAN
Chandni RESTAU

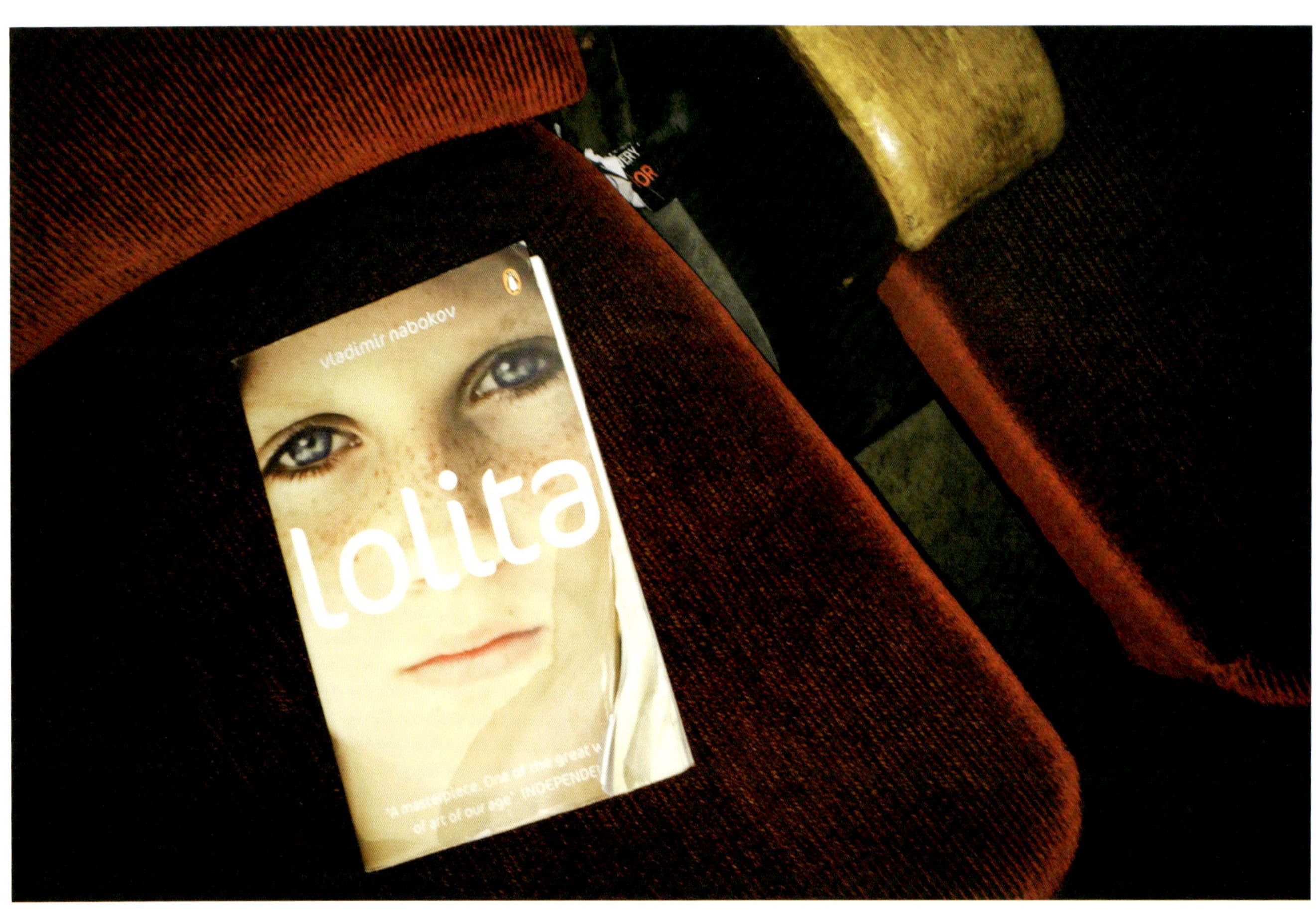
vladimir nabokov
lolita

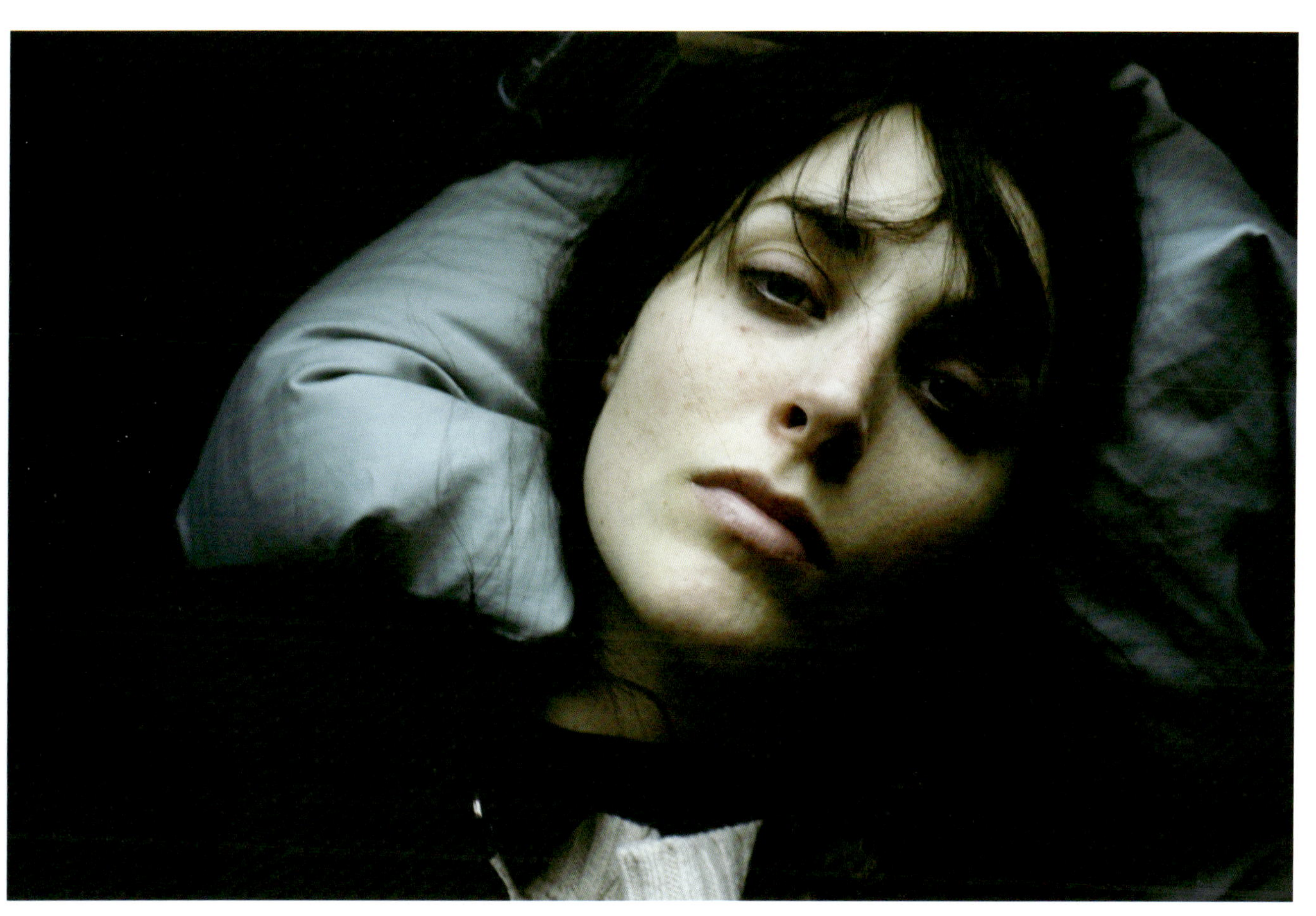

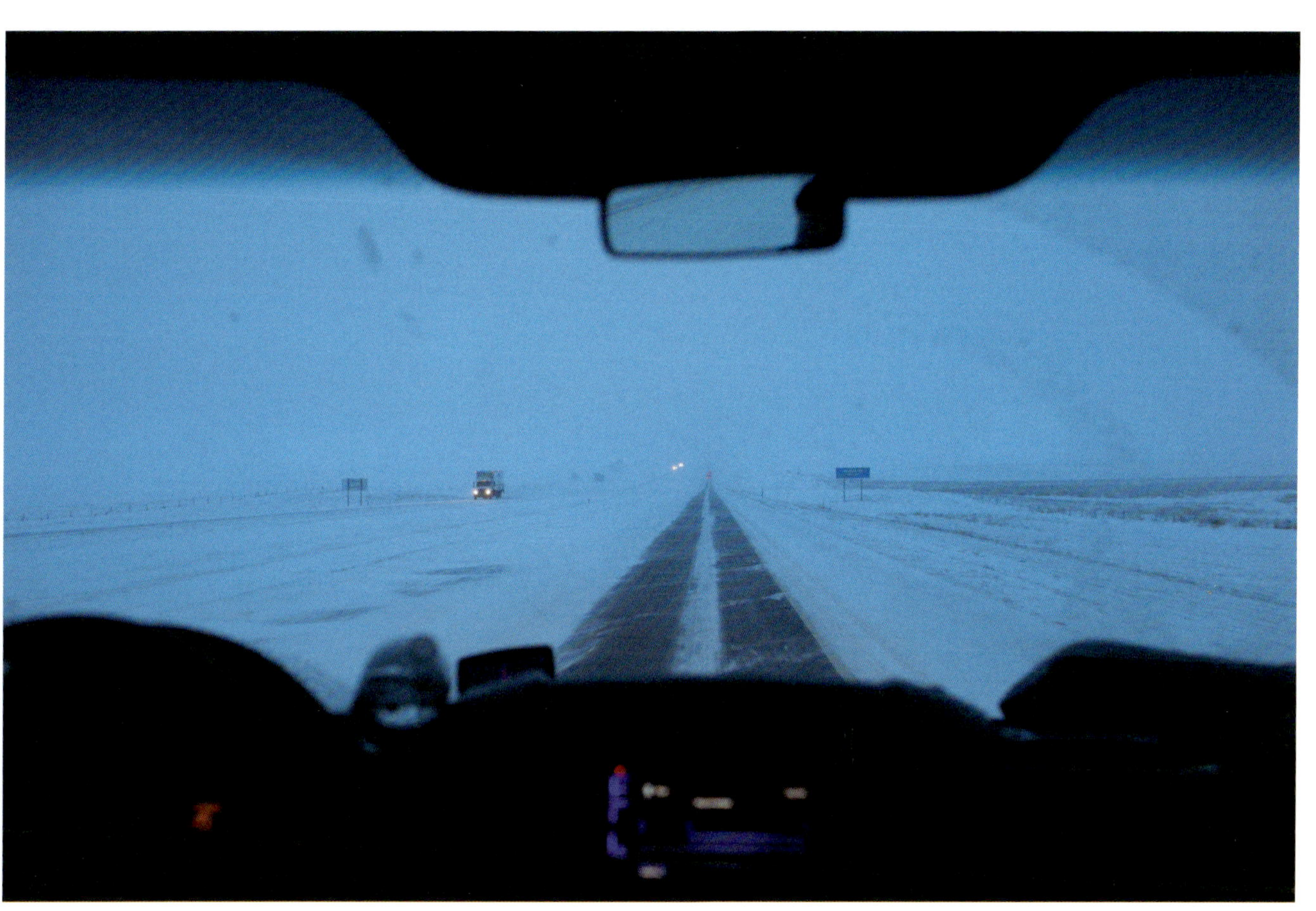

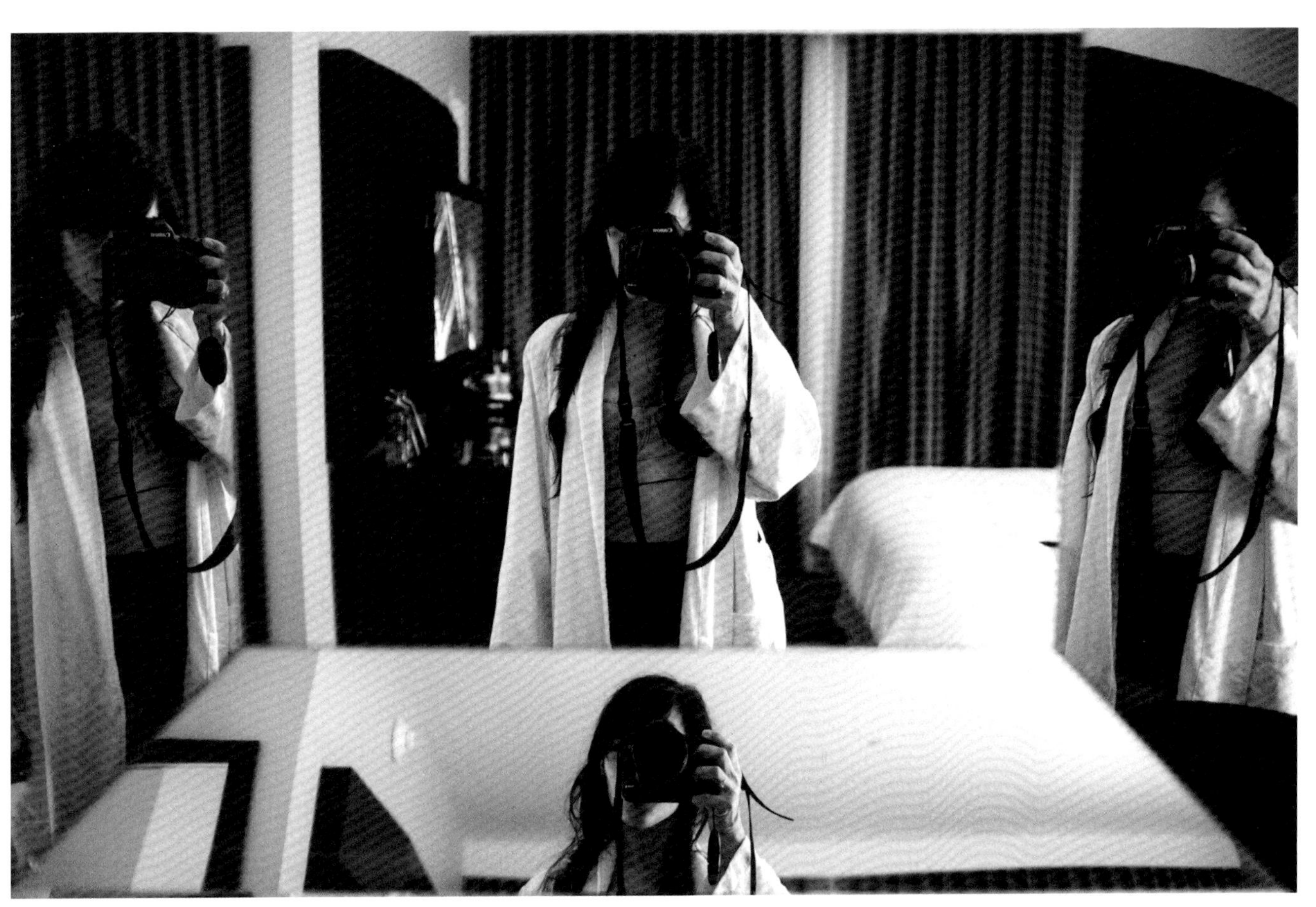

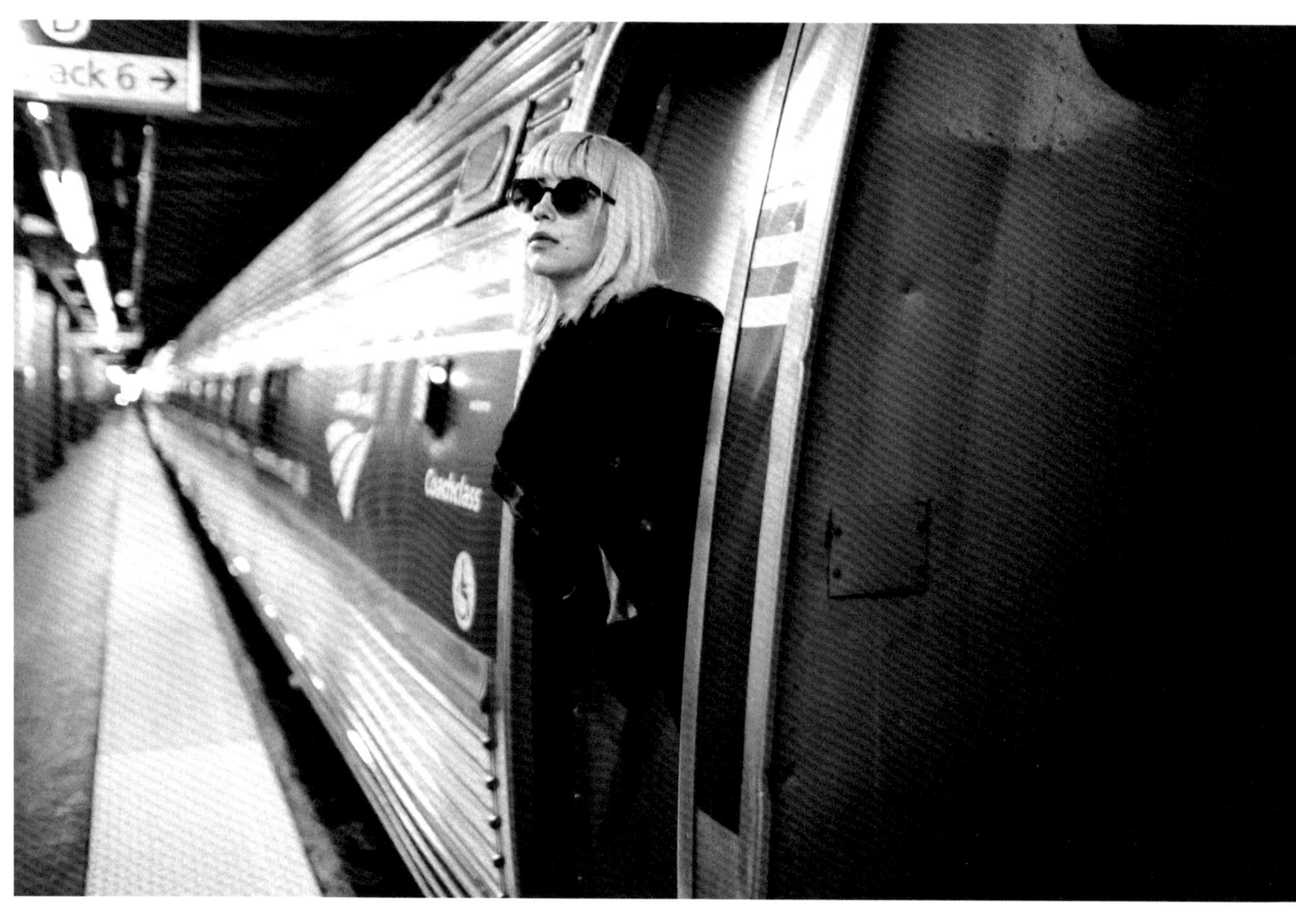
ack 6 →

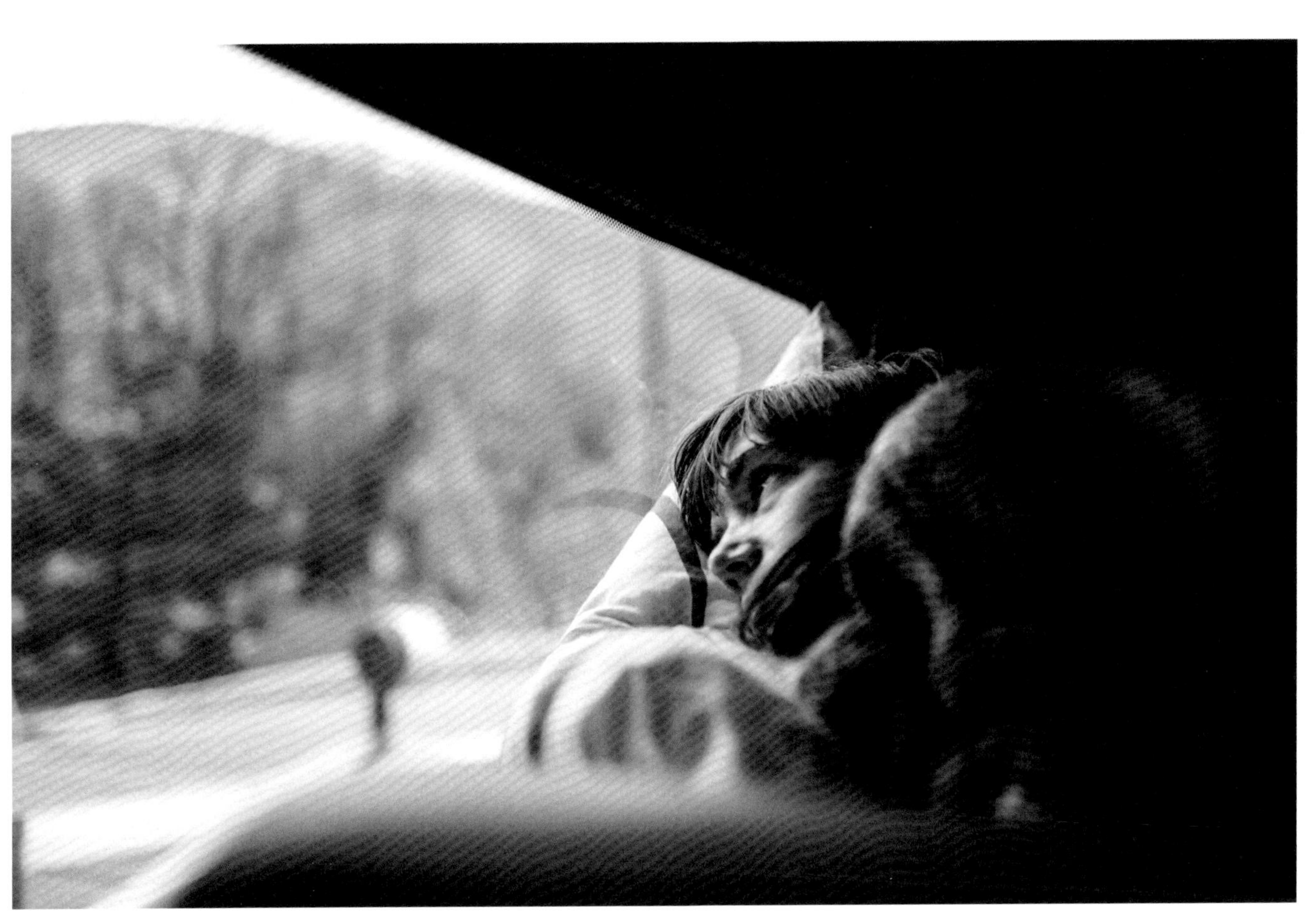

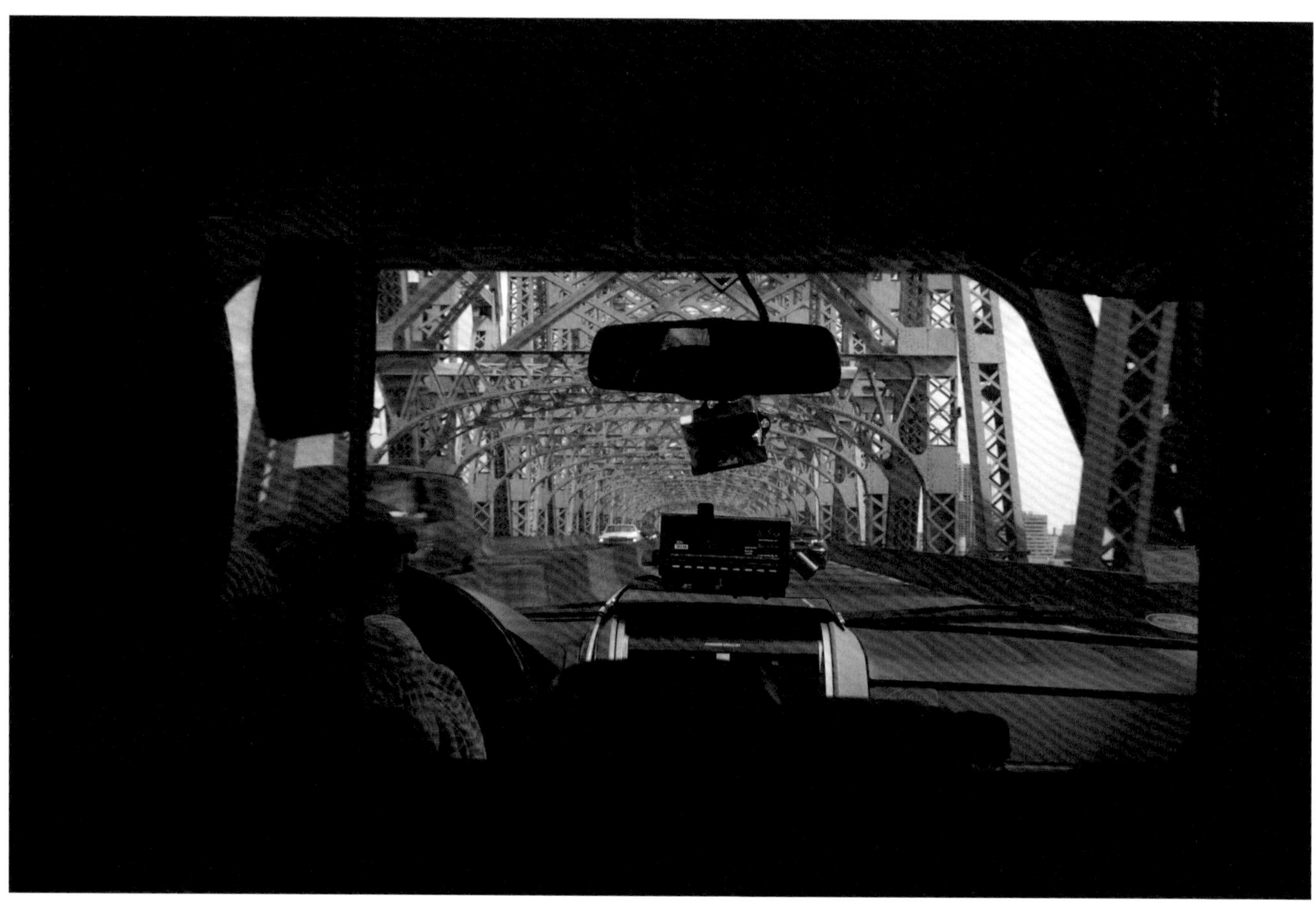

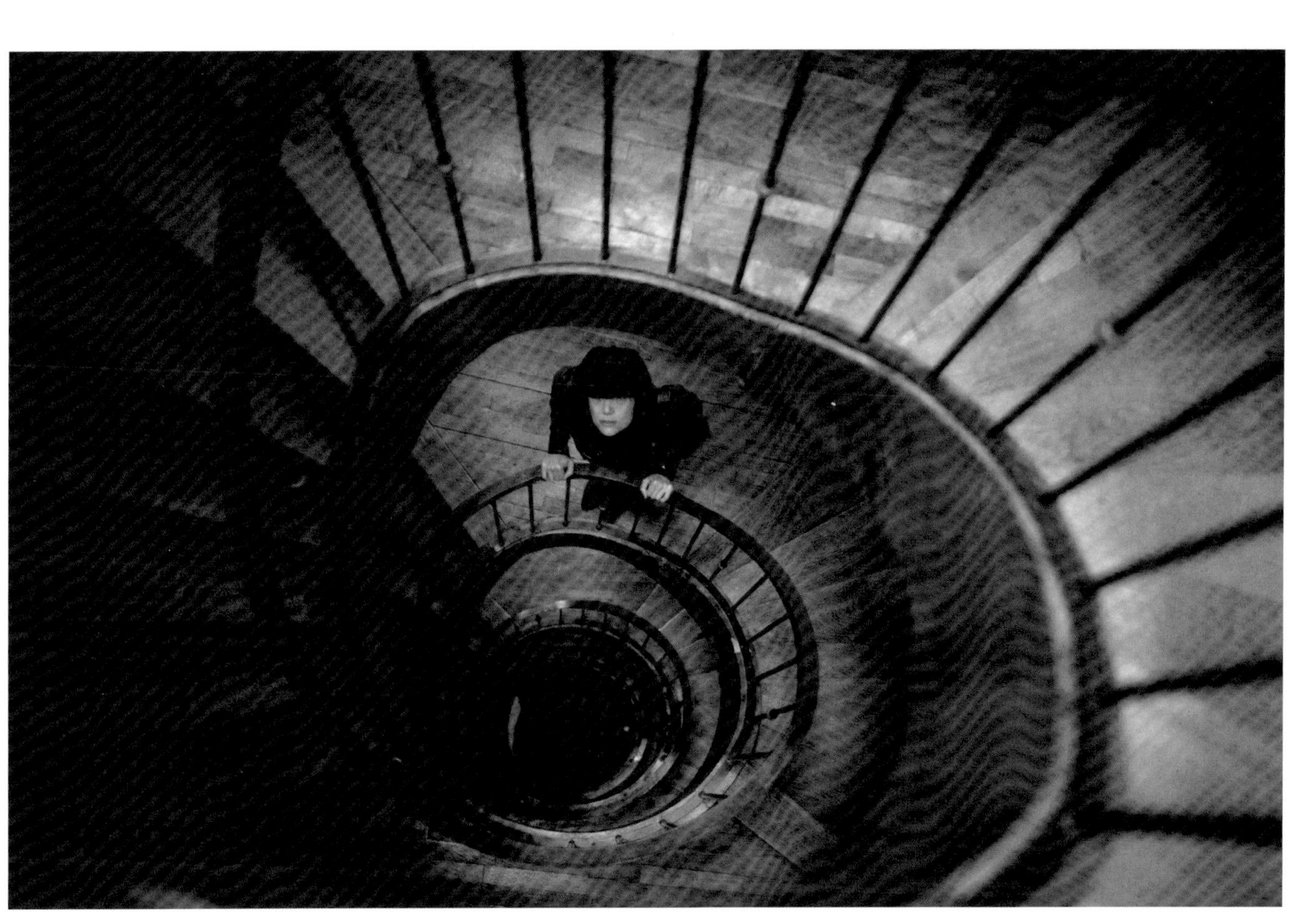

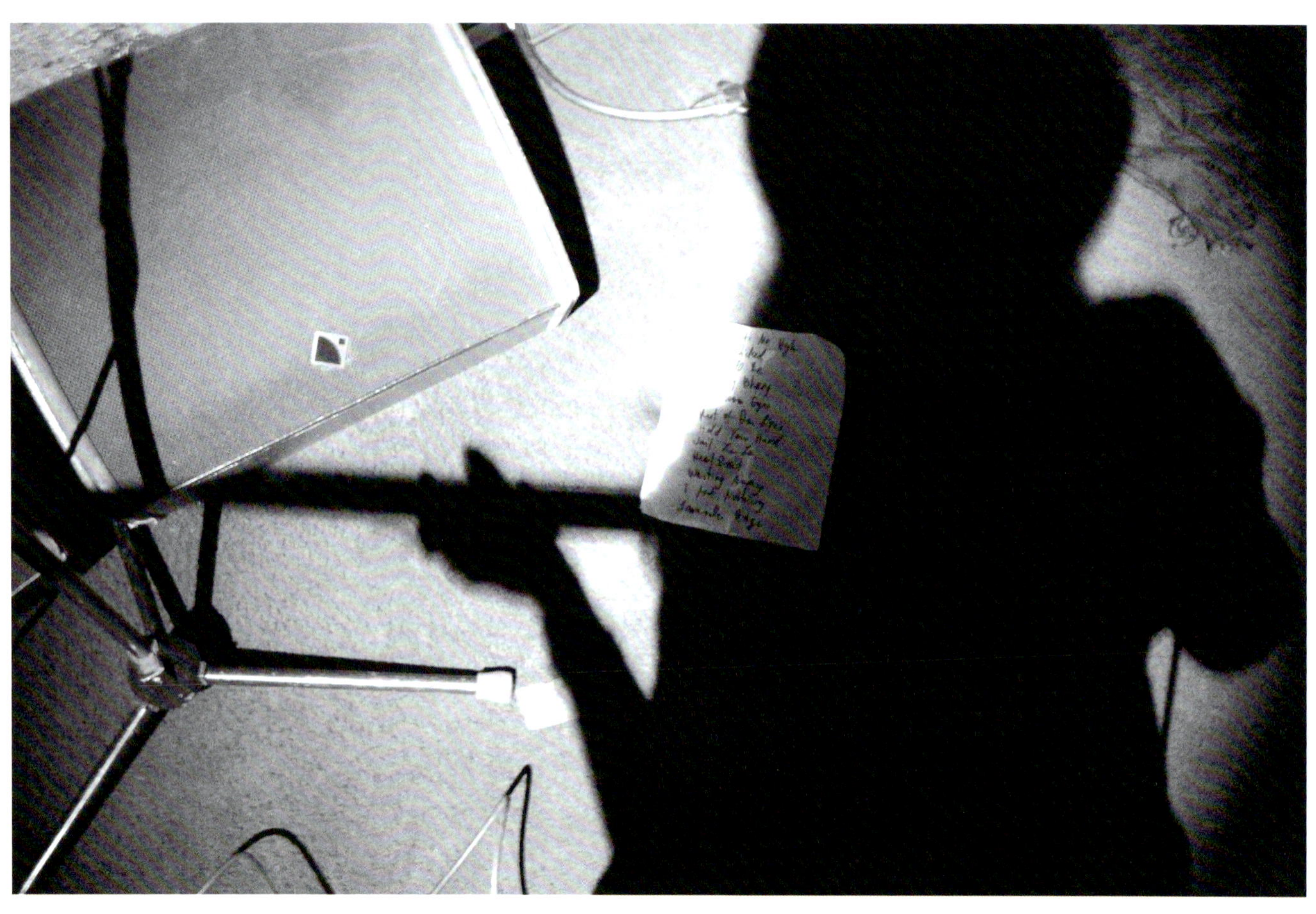

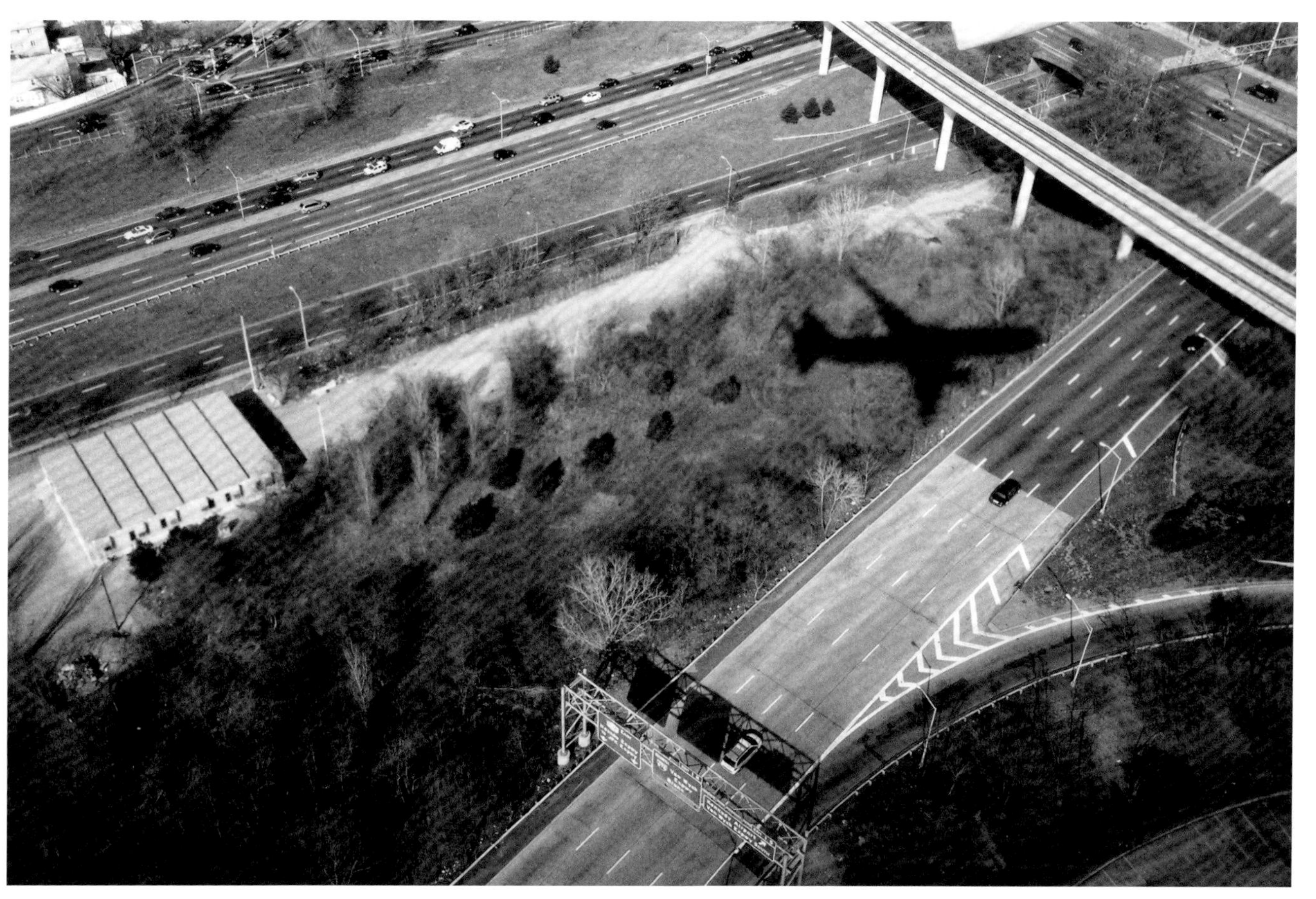

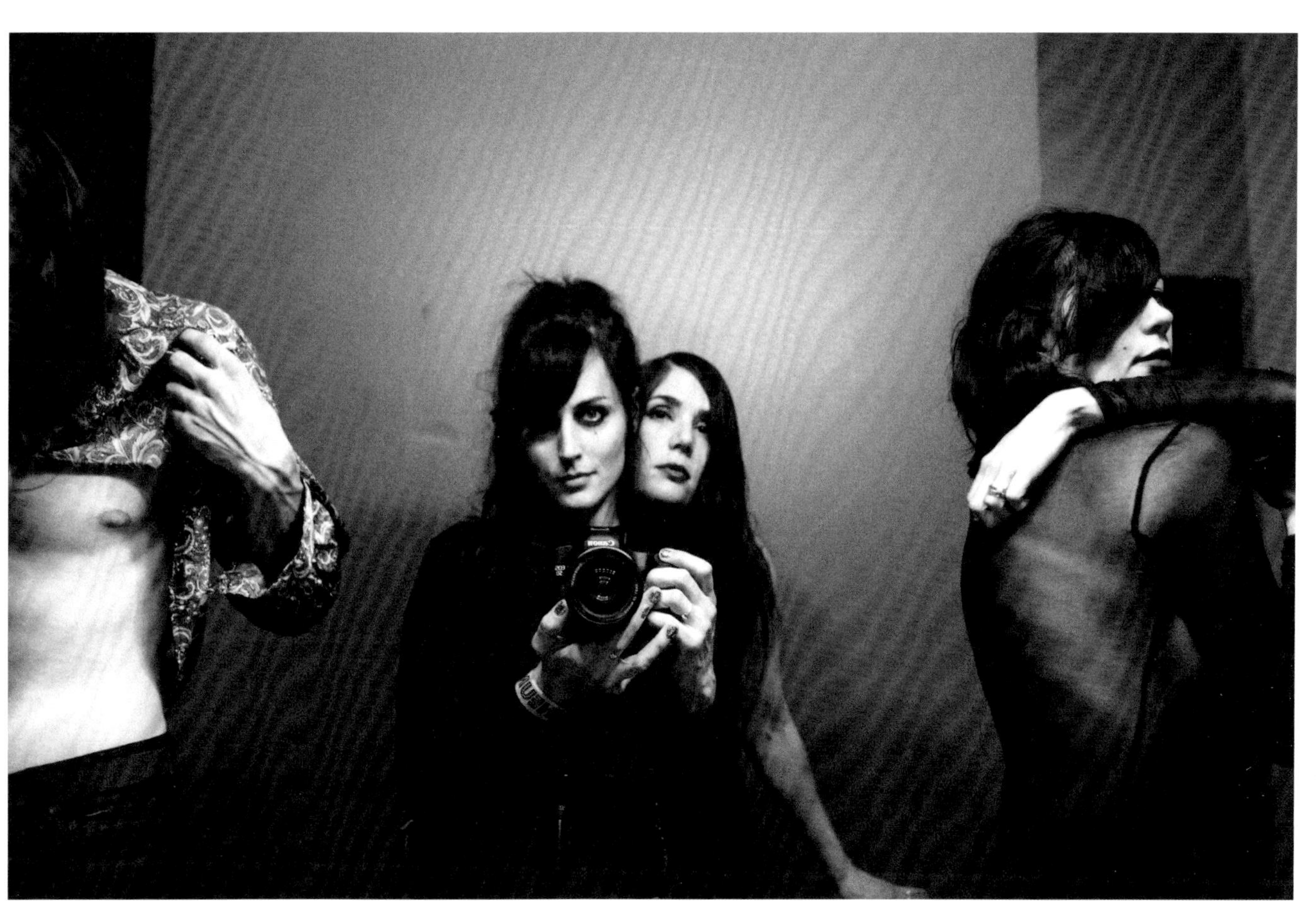

AFTERWORD

Pulling these together after so much time off the road brought up a lot of feelings. I lived the life I'd always dreamt of having, but at the time, I was often so tired or felt so untethered, I wasn't really enjoying it. Even knowing the album cycle for *Too True* would be my last, I still didn't soak it up. I didn't think how it would really feel to put my bass down forever. To never shuffle my bags downstairs for lobby call. To never look across the stage from me and share a smile with my bandmates. To hear the roar of the crowd or to look out and see those faces smiling back at me.

If you've wanted to be in a band but never tired, try it. Go for it. Stop dating musicians and stop idolizing them. Become one. And if you're on the road, enjoy every moment of it because someday it'll all be over.

MALIA JAMES AND NICK ZINNER

Nick Zinner of Yeah Yeah Yeahs and Malia James met on tour and connected over being both photographers and musicians. They presented a two-person photo shoot in Los Angeles called "Everywhere and Nowhere in Between," which featured one hundred images by each artist from their time on tour. Below is a conversation between them regarding the intentions behind this book.

MALIA: Hi, Nick! I was always really inspired by how you were able to hover the line and be both an image and music maker.

NICK: Ahh, thanks, Malia, that's lovely to hear. It's been really awesome to watch your recent artistic evolution(s).

MALIA: Do you recall how we first met?

NICK: Was it after a Dum Dum Girls show in New York, and we all went to a weird hotel party on the west side? I've got a terrible memory, but I'm thinking that was it. Let's get the basic stuff out of the way—when and how did you first start taking photos?

MALIA: My first memory was a trip to Disneyland with my grandfather at age eight. I shot fourteen rolls of film. He was lovingly furious and didn't understand how someone could take that many photos, but I always remember that as the first time I was really looking at the world around me and seeing frames.

NICK: What made you continue?

MALIA: How does the saying go? "This life chose me…"? I have, for most of my life, felt propelled by an unquenchable thirst to create.

MALIA: Were you taking photos before playing music?

NICK: I took my first photo class in my junior year of high school but was playing guitar in my room starting around sixth grade. But then again I did just find negatives of myself as a six-year-old with a little point-and-shoot.

MALIA : Was there ever a time you thought you'd only pursue one professionally?

NICK: I went through different times when I first moved to New York City where I tried to do both professionally, but failed horribly. I decided that I would just do both only for myself and just try to work with whatever skills I had, like for the first few years after college I worked in darkrooms as a printer, right up until the first Yeah Yeah Yeahs record was recorded. But I was documenting everything around me the whole time. Do you shoot film or digital?

MALIA: I was one of the last photographers I know to transition to digital when that became the way, but now I enjoy it. I like to alternate between the two, but I prefer the speed at which I can process digital files. Nothing compares to the texture and tones you get from film, though.

NICK: What or who was your first visual inspiration?

MALIA: For imagery, the first photographer I remember exploring deeper was Mary Ellen Mark. *Seven* was the first movie that made me outwardly proclaim I wanted to be a director. *American Beauty* solidified that feeling.

MALIA: Who are some of your influences visually?

NICK: I love the classic *Magnum* documentary photographers like Cartier-Bresson and Elliot Erwitt, and also Robert Frank and William Klein. But I was also influenced by more conceptual artists like Sophie Calle and Bernd and Hilla Becher. How did you come to join Dum Dum Girls?

MALIA:I came to music late in life.

NICK: When you were touring and playing music, did you see your shooting as documenting your life or were you using it as another creative tool?

MALIA: There's a big difference in the images I took as a photographer on tour and when I was documenting my life as a musician. Suddenly, I was on the inside, looking out. I would definitely say I was documenting my life, but there are so many moments you miss because you're *in them*. My therapist would say that's a good thing—being in the moment—but it means maybe I missed making some iconic images. When I was a tour photographer, I was mostly interested in the people around me. When it was me capturing my own experience, I was more interested in the spaces we passed through. While the internet has ruined the legacy of a self-portrait by the birth of the "selfie," I was documenting myself in these places as a journal entry. A check in with myself along the way. Looking back on them, they're the most effective documentation.

NICK: I often feel like when you are photographing things personal to you , you are essentially writing your own history or memory. Do you feel the same?

MALIA: If my photographs are my memoir, I've left more unsaid than I put on paper. I have a horrible memory, so at times the pictures are my way of remembering.

NICK: Are you still shooting photographs?

MALIA: It feels like every minute of my twenties were documented and my thirties are almost entirely undocumented except screenshots of memes. I have had this realization many times over the last few years, but haven't actually starting documenting things as much again. Maybe today is the day. Is photo more important to you now?

NICK: In some ways it is. As I've become older and seen so much change and loss, having a visual and personal record of past experience and times is proving to be more and more precious. Do you feel overwhelmed by the overabundance of imagery these days, and have you noticed a shift? How does that affect you if so?

MALIA: Sometimes it feels like the more I consume, the less I'm creating.

NICK: What made you want to get into video?

MALIA: Directing is and was always my ultimate goal. At fourteen, my school didn't have a film program, so I got into theater and photography as a way to build my eye and develop an understanding of performance. There was a period when I thought I felt there were too many people involved in film and I wanted something that I could just go out and do on my own in that moment. What can't be captured in an image but heard in music?

NICK: The sound of one hand clapping. Do you still wish you were in a band?

MALIA: Yes and no. The idea of never playing a show again breaks my heart a little. I've recently been toying with the idea of doing another run with a band, but it would all need to fall into place. It'd have to be the right music and timing and not take away from directing too much.

NICK: Were you aware when taking these photos that many of them would be taken on your last tour with that band?

MALIA: I knew it was my last album cycle, yes. I felt I had delayed pursuing my true passion—directing—for too long, and it was time to put all of my energy into that one task. There's a part of me that was still in denial, I think. Looking back on it, I wasn't enjoying or capturing the final chapter of my life in a way I would have wished. Also, I wasn't shooting with the intention of making a book. I think I'd have shot something differently if I'd been out there "on assignment."

NICK: When I meet younger musicians in bands, I always encourage them to document their experiences as everything is fleeting, and not just with their phones. What do you feel the camera captures that the phone or Instagram can't?

MALIA: I agree with the saying that whatever camera you have on you is best. The images in this book were taken on various different cameras—from my 5D, Contax T3, and my phone. I think Instagram and phone cameras have ruined photography in a way because we're overdocumenting the mundane everyday instead of looking for images and moments.

INDEX

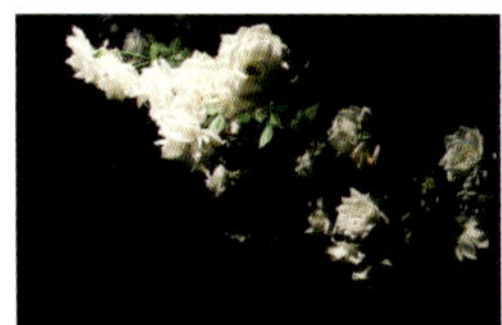

NIGHT FLOWERS
/ Page 70

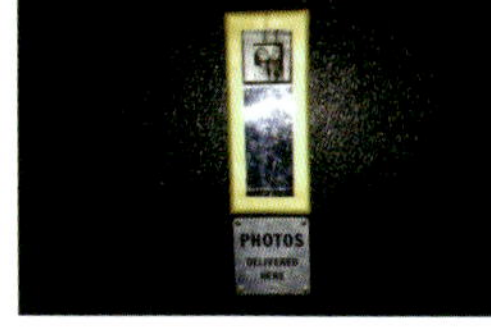

ANDREW AND I
/ Page 71

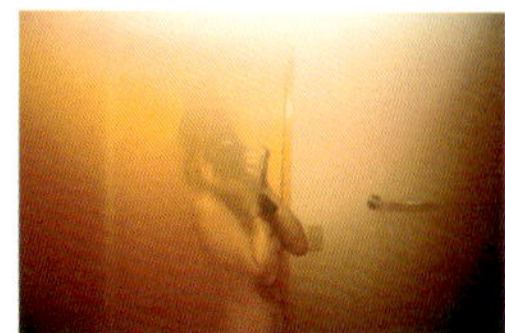

NUDE COACHELLA
/ Page 72

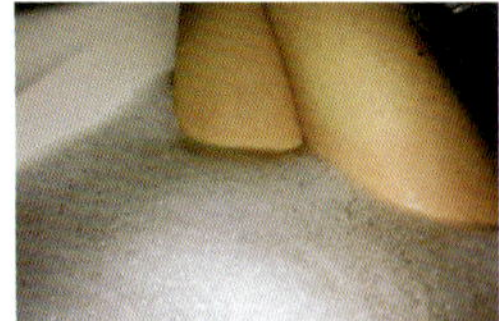

FOR HIM
/ Page 73

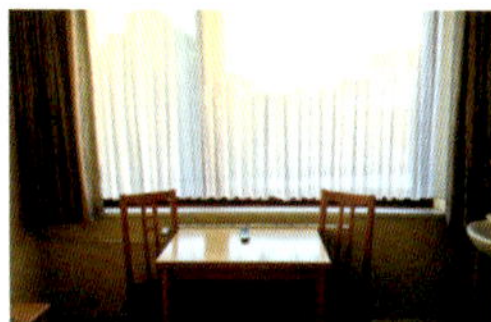

WHERE WE SMOKED
/ Page 74

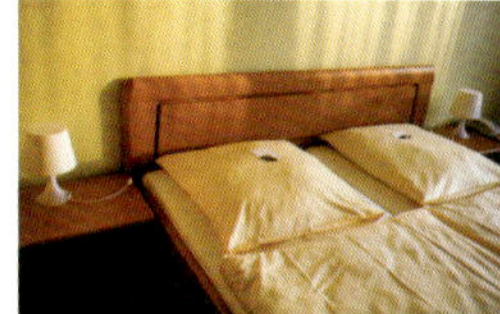

A BED WE HAD SEX IN
/ Page 75

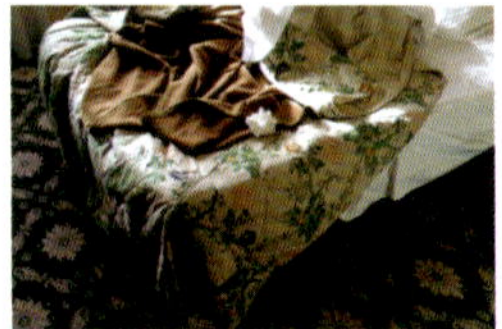

WHERE WE BROKE UP, MI-
LAN / Page 76

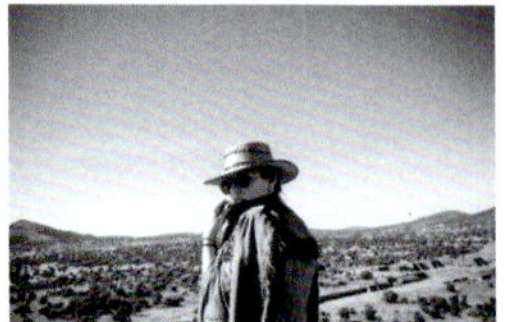

DANA IN MEXICO
/ Page 79

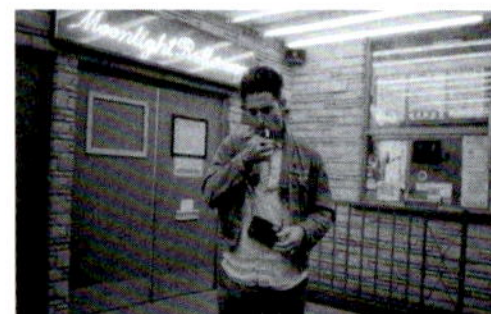

MOONLIGHT
/ Page 80

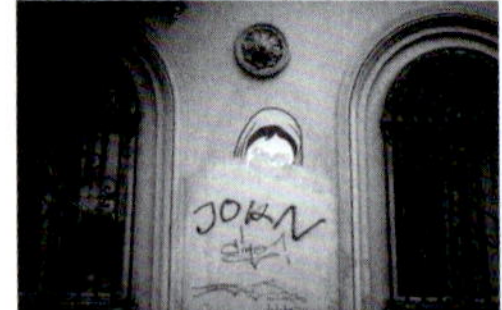

FACELESS WOMAN
/ Page 82

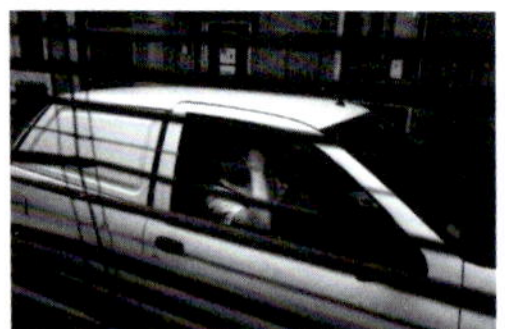

PASSING THROUGH
/ Page 83

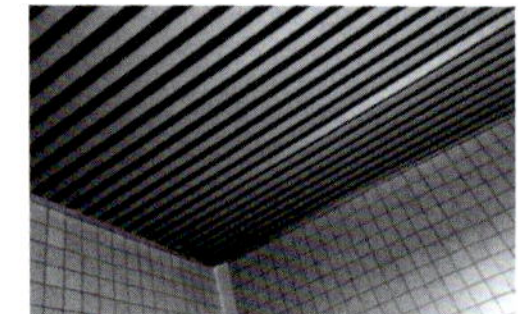

PARIS
/ Page 84

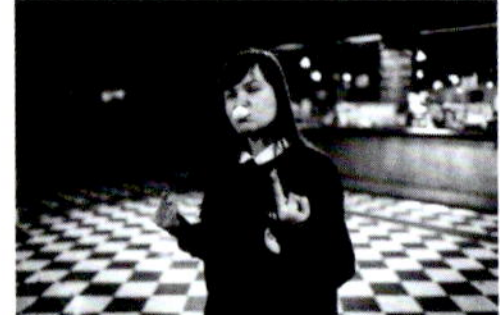

F U
/ Page 85

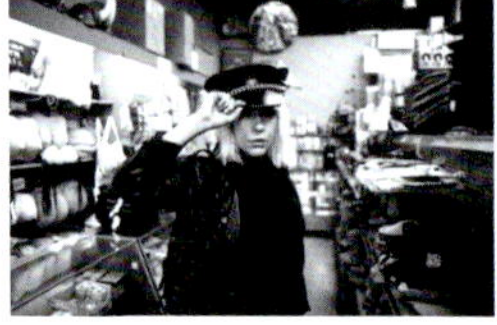

DEE DEE COP
/ Page 86

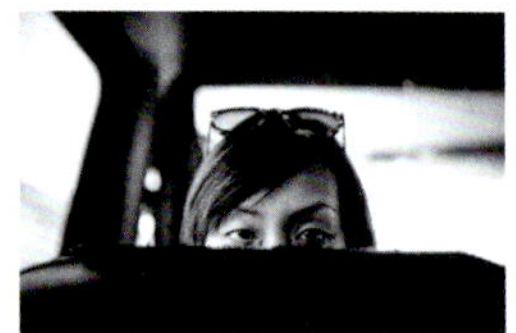

SANDY VAN
/ Page 87

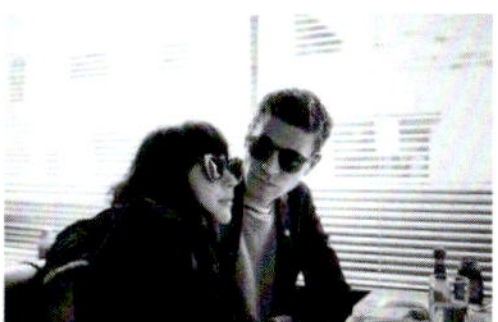

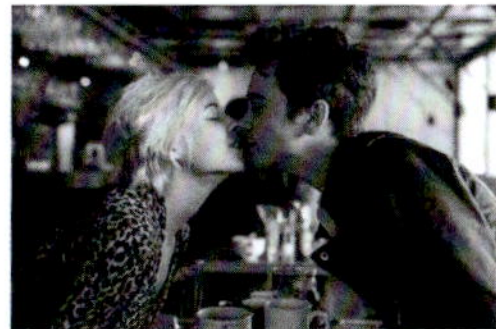

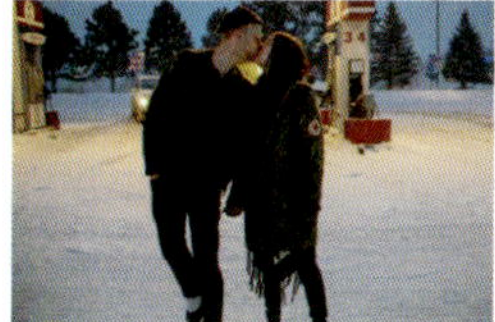

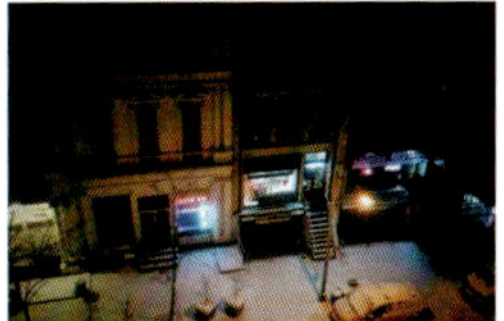

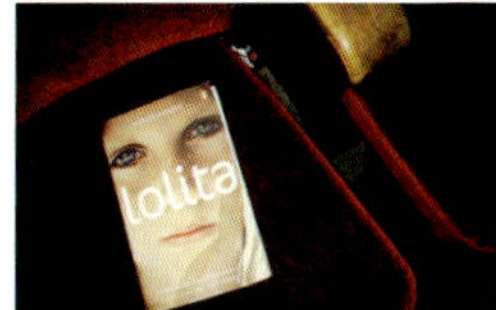
lolita

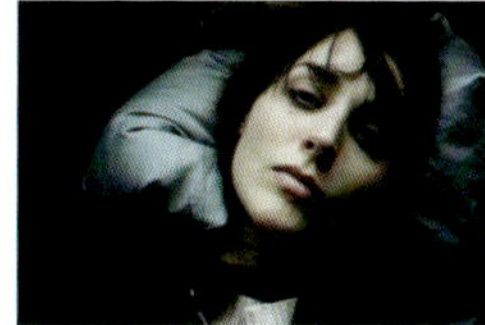

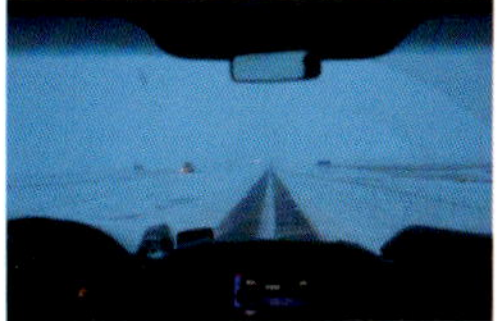

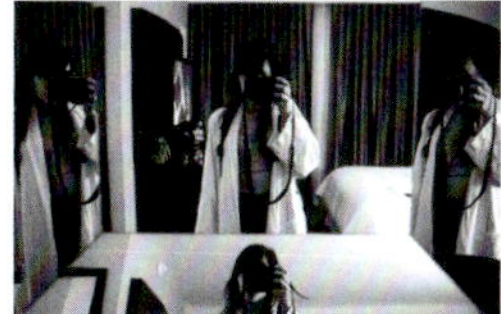

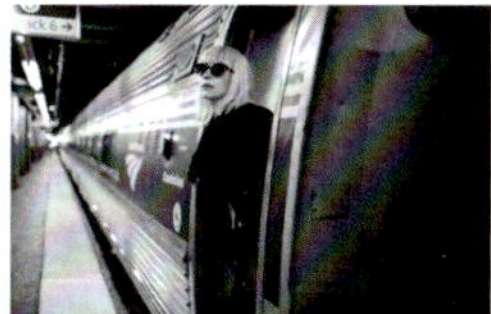

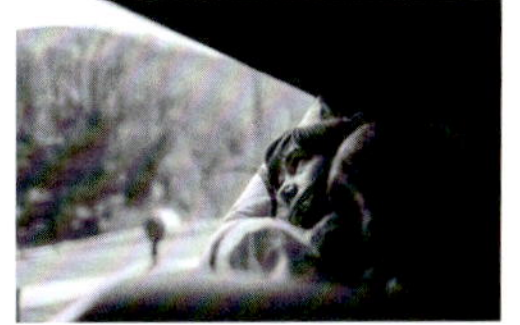

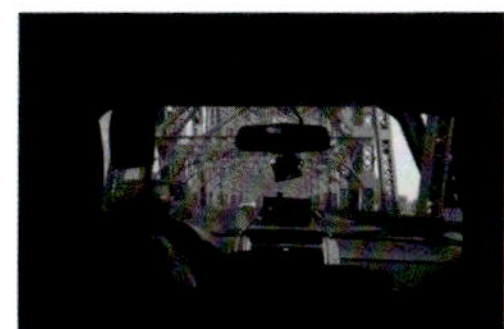

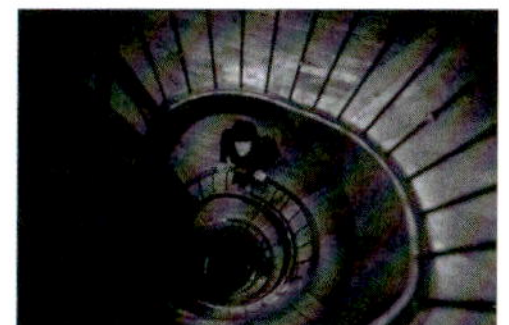

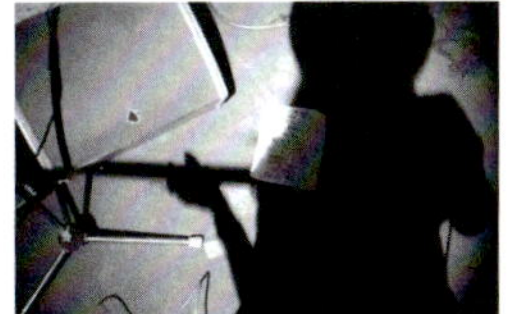

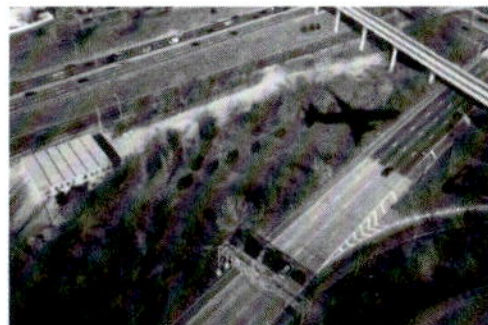

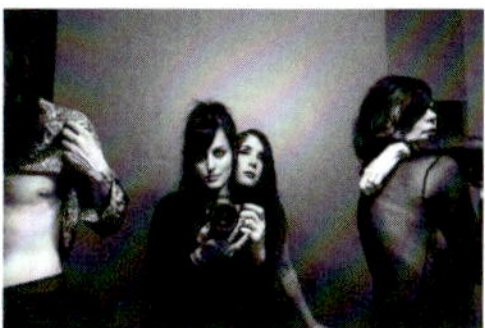

THIS IS A GENUINE RARE BIRD BOOK

A Rare Bird Book | Rare Bird Books
453 South Spring Street, Suite 302
Los Angeles, CA 90013
rarebirdbooks.com

FIRST HARDCOVER EDITION

For more information, address:
Rare Bird Books Subsidiary Rights Department
453 South Spring Street, Suite 302
Los Angeles, CA 90013

Set in Sofia
Printed in Canada

10 9 8 7 6 5 4 3 2 1

Publisher's Cataloging-in-Publication Data
available on request

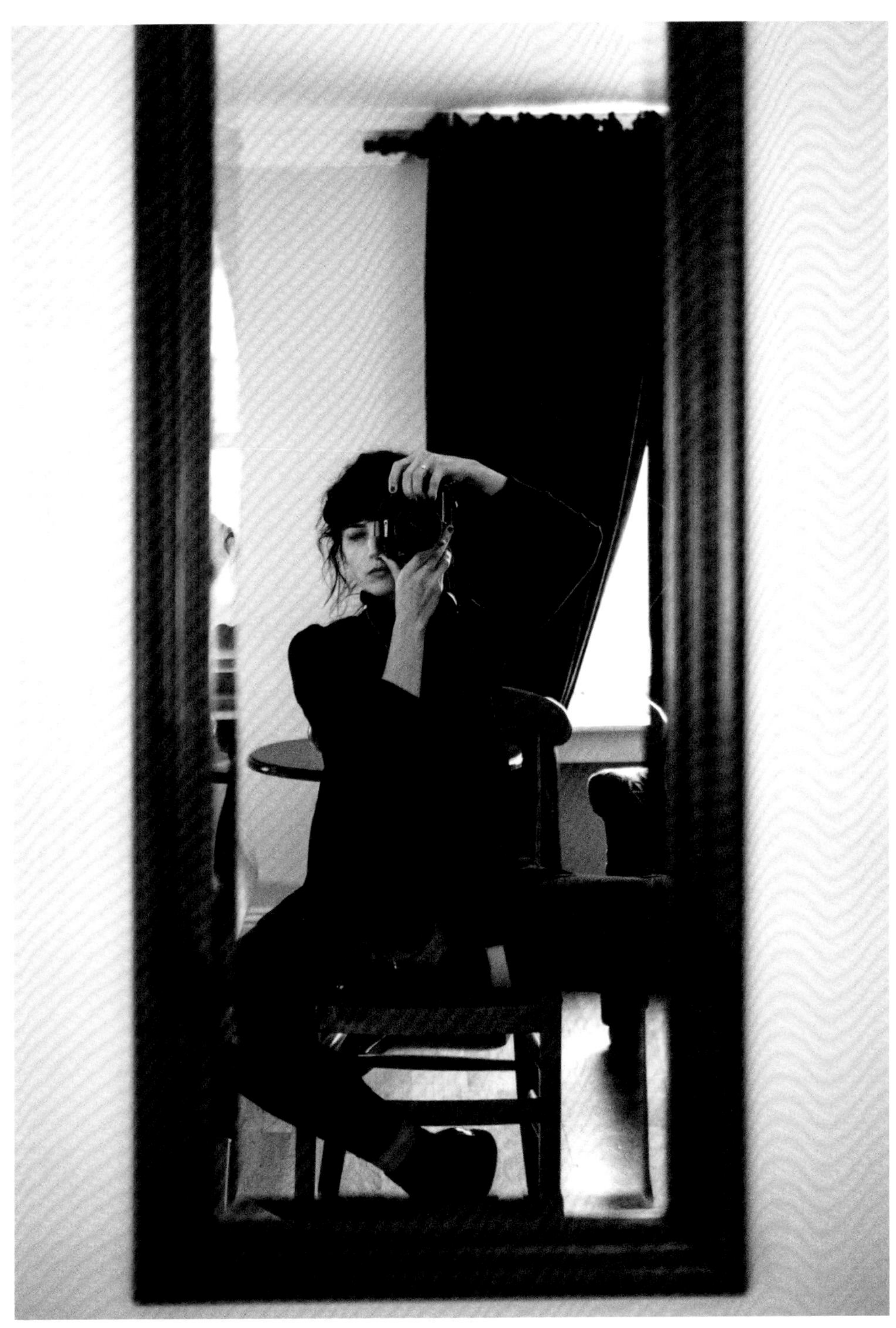